GAMES

Compiled by
Mary Hohenstein

BETHANY HOUSE PUBLISHERS
MINNEAPOLIS, MINNESOTA 55438

Published by Bethany House Publishers
A Ministry of Bethany Fellowship International
11400 Hampshire Avenue South
Minneapolis, Minnesota 55438
www.bethanyhouse.com

Printed in the United States of America by
Bethany Press International, Minneapolis, Minnesota 55438

ISBN 0–7642–2321–6

The Library of Congress has cataloged a previous edition of this book as follows:

Hohenstein, Mary.
    Games.

    Includes index.
    1. Games. I. Work of Christ Community. II. Title
GV1203.H563   794   80–23047
ISBN 0–87123–191–3

Compiler's Note

I am not actually what you would call the author of this book. In fact, in the literal sense I am not even the sole compiler! Many considerations and factors come into play, however, in the publication of a book, and several of these have combined to place my name on the cover of this book as the "compiler." Actually, this book was both written and compiled by the entire Work of Christ Community, a Christian community comprised of approximately 650 men, women, and children in Lansing and East Lansing, Michigan. Members of this ecumenical community are men and women of different ages, denominations and stages of life. Families and single people, working men and students, older and younger—all share a common commitment to live for the Lord Jesus fully and be formed together as a people for God.

In addition to a common life together of praise and worship, service, fellowship, receiving teaching, and forming deeper relationships of Christian love with one another, the community life includes recreation, parties, picnics and entertainment. It is from these times of recreation together that this book has emerged.

The community is organized geographically into districts, which are composed of 75-150 adults. Each district frequently comes together for parties or picnics. Thus, games or activities for large groups are used or created. Within each district, the brothers and sisters are arranged into small groups of families and single people. These small groups have weekly times of fellowship and recreation. These times together have generated many creative activities and games for small groups. The children participate in the community's Youth Activities Program. They get together each Saturday for a craft, sport, or other activity, enabling them to have fun together and build relationships. Many of the games for children or teens in this book were contributed by Youth Activity workers in The Work of Christ Community.

Games is the product of a major effort by the entire community. As stated earlier, hundreds of people in a variety of different situations contributed games and ideas. Some are popular, traditional games that have been passed on for years. Others are original, created by community members as they explored new ways to recreate and have a fun evening together. Some are variations of old games, adapting them to the family or Christian setting.

Although the contributors of games were given the same forms to fill out to describe their games or activities, it took hours of labor by a number of persons in the community with writing and secretarial skills to rewrite each game in a uniform, clear format. They also organized the games into categories, indexed them, typed them and mimeographed them. The compilation was then distributed to community members and the games and activities were used throughout the group for two years. After the games had been thoroughly "tested and tried," before final publication, all community members were asked to submit any revisions or variations they had developed, any suggestions for ways to write any of the games more clearly and any new games or activities they had created in the last two years. These were then integrated into the book.

As we prepared the book for publication, we found that we needed an individual's name for the cover. (It would be impossible to list all the contributors from The Work of Christ Community.) My name was chosen, as I have been involved with the work since its inception. It should be abundantly clear, however, that this book is a joint project of the whole Community.

The members of The Work of Christ Community hope that this book will serve other Christians. Due to the relationship-oriented nature of the community, with its emphasis on family life, as well as coming together with other families and single people, this game book is especially applicable for Christians who want to gather with other Christians, enjoy one another, and deepen their relationships as they relax and have fun together.

Mary Hohenstein

Note: Those who would like to learn more about our life together are welcome to visit The Work of Christ Community. Arrangements can be made by writing: Guestmaster, The Work of Christ Community, P.O. Box 392, East Lansing, Michigan 48823.

A companion volume, *Noncompetitive Games for People of All Ages*, is also available.

Table of Contents

PHYSICALLY ACTIVE GAMES

Large Open Area

Races and Relays

Tag, Team Tag, and Capture Games

Traditional Sports with a Twist

CREATIVE-DRAMATIC GAMES

Artistic Games

Dramatic Games

Musical Games

Storytelling Games

RELATIONSHIP-BUILDING GAMES

Getting-To-Know-Each-Other Games

Games of Encouragement and Edification

GUESSING GAMES

Games in Which One Person Guesses

Making the Others Guess

WORD, THINKING, AND QUIET GAMES

Word Games

Paper-and-Pencil Thinking Games

Quiet Circle Games

MISCELLANEOUS

Trip Games

Card Games

Card Games—for use with Rook ® deck

A Homemade Board Game

Party Games

Traveling Games

FAMILY AND FELLOWSHIP ACTIVITIES
Quiet Evenings at Home

Celebrations and Special Dinners

Outings

CHILDREN'S GAMES AND ACTIVITY IDEAS

Outdoor Activities

Introduction

This collection of games and activities is a valuable resource for Christian families, church groups or fellowships, those who work with children or teens, and any others who plan recreational activities for adults and children in Christian settings.

The book is written and organized in a way to make it an easy, handy reference for planning. The games are categorized by "kind" or type, to help you find the type of game you are looking for. Such categorizing is difficult as categories may overlap; one game may fit into several different categories, or one game may not fit exactly into any particular category. Alphabetical and topical indices of all the games in the book are provided in the back to further help you in locating a game. A cross reference is provided in each index, i.e., a familiar game title is listed, followed in parentheses by its title in this book. Also, a popular variation of a game is listed, followed in parentheses by its actual game title.

Each game is explained in a uniform format, with information and instructions for playing the game fully stated. The number of players, length of time, materials needed, physical arrangements, preparation required, object of the game, and procedure for playing are described in a concise, clear manner. Variations on a game and special comments about it may also be given. The purpose or benefit of each game is also stated. It should be noted, however, that rules will vary from group to group. The length of time, number of players, and other factors can be extremely variable. Therefore, the rules for each game should be regarded as *suggested* guidelines.

The games in this book have been selected as appropriate for Christian recreational situations. Some are just fun activities to do together; others are obviously designed to help people get to know one another better, encourage each other, and build deeper relationships. Most games have the element of competition, often the primary characteristic of a "game." Competition in games can be approached by Christians with an attitude of brotherly love, thus increasing enjoyment and excitement, without creating contention, strife, wrong speech, or negative feelings about oneself. Many of the games included require cooperation and teamwork; they encourage communication and positive interaction, stimulate creativity and alert thinking, develop increased physical coordination or dexterity. The main purpose of all the games is to help individuals recreate and have fun together.

Another section of the book describes various activities (not essentially games) that Christian groups or families may enjoy doing together. This can be a valuable resource in planning recreational activities. There is also a special section of activities for children and youth groups. It should be noted that other than this section, no distinction is made between games appropriate for adults or children. It may be mentioned that adults or children may enjoy a particular game more, and some are obviously more appropriate for one group than another; but most of the games can be played by either adults or children, or both.

PHYSICALLY ACTIVE GAMES

Many of these games need to be played *outdoors* or in a large *indoor area*. Some are more physically active than others. This section is divided into five sub-sections.

Large Open Area Games
Races and Relays
Tag, Team Tag and Capture Games
Traditional Sports with a Twist
Ball Games—Of All Kinds

Many of these games are popular *picnic games* for large groups. This section also contains traditional *children's games*. There are also many new and creative tags and relays which children and/or adults enjoy.

Balloon Toss

Number of Players:	8-30
Length of Time:	10-15 minutes
Materials:	A small balloon filled with water for every 2 players
Playing Site:	Large open outdoor area
Preparation:	Players should dress to get.wet. Fill balloons with water.
Object of the Game:	To be the last pair with an unbroken balloon.

To Play:

Everyone finds a partner. The players stand in two rows, partners facing each other about three feet apart. The players in one row each have a balloon. At a signal, the balloons are tossed to the partners in the other row who carefully catch them.

Everyone then takes a step back and the balloons are returned. This procedure is repeated as many times as necessary.

A couple is eliminated when their balloon breaks. The last two players remaining are the winners.

Variation:

A more expensive and messy version of the game uses eggs instead of balloons.

Purpose or Benefit

This is a popular picnic contest. It is also a fun way to cool off on a hot day!

Bola

Number of Players:	5-15
Length of Time:	10-20 minutes
Materials:	A "Bola" is made by stuffing a rubber softball into a long sock. A knot is tied in the sock just above the ball. A clothesline rope is securely tied to the sock. The rope should be at least 12 feet long.
Playing Site:	A large open area
Object of the Game:	To successfully jump the Bola.

To Play:

One player lies down on his back and starts spinning the Bola, slowly letting out the rope.

When the rope reaches a good radius (about 12 feet), the other players begin jumping over the Bola/rope.

As the players get used to jumping, the spinner can speed up.

Variation:

People can try jumping in pairs or with everyone holding hands.

Purpose or Benefit

This is a good picnic game. There is no competition and all ages can participate.

Cat-and-Mouse Trap

Number of Players:	10-20
Length of Time:	30-60 minutes
Playing Site:	Large open area
Object of the Game:	To be the last mouse not caught in the "trap."

To Play:

Five people are chosen to be the "trap" and form a circle by holding hands with arms raised over their heads.

One person is chosen to be the "cat," who starts by facing away from the trap, *not* looking at it (perhaps with eyes closed).

The remaining players are all "mice."

The game begins with the mice walking in and out of the trap simultaneously.

The cat waits for the right moment and then suddenly turns back around and shouts "Snap!" at which point the trap brings its arms down and captures whoever is in the circle. The captured mice become part of the trap.

The game continues until all but one mouse is caught. He is declared the winner (and gets the cheese)!

Purpose or Benefit

"Cat-and-Mouse Trap" is a suspenseful, dramatic game especially enjoyed by young children.

Catch the Dragon's Tail

Number of Players:	10-30
Length of Time:	15-45 minutes
Materials:	A large scarf or handkerchief
Playing Site:	Large open area
Object of the Game:	The first person in the line tries to catch the last person in line.

To Play:

All the players line up and put their hands on the waist of the person in front of them. The last person in line tucks one end of the scarf in his back pocket, belt, or waistband. The first person in line tries to grab the scarf. When the "head" gets the "tail," he dons the scarf and becomes the new tail. The person second in line becomes the new head.

Variation:

Form two or more teams, each being a "dragon" trying to catch the others' tails.

Purpose or Benefit

This is a good game for picnics or big gatherings. There is no winner or loser.

Greased Watermelon Polo

Number of Players:	8-20
Length of Time	15-60 minutes
Materials:	One watermelon One pound of lard (or other type of grease) Buoys (if playing in a lake)
Playing Site:	Lake or swimming pool
Preparation:	Spread lard over the surface of a watermelon. If playing in a lake, position buoys to delineate the boundaries of the playing area. Dimensions should be approximately 15 yards x 20 yards. Each team then selects one of the two end lines as its goal.
Object of the Game:	For a team to carry the watermelon over its designated goal more times than the opposing team succeeds in carrying it over its goal.

To Play:

Participants are divided into two equal teams. Both teams line up facing each other in the middle of the playing area. One player carries the watermelon in between the two teams and drops it at any point he wishes. The teams battle for possession of the watermelon and attempt to move it toward their respective goals.

One point is awarded to a team whenever the watermelon crosses its goal.

After a point is scored, play is resumed with the teams lining up for a face-off as at the beginning.

If the watermelon crosses one of the sidelines, the teams line up for a face-off at the point where the watermelon went out-of-bounds.

Length of the game should be twenty minutes, or else the first team to score ten points.

Variation:

To increase the amount of action, use more than one watermelon. This is especially appropriate for large groups.

Comments:

When playing in a swimming pool, players should consider that lard does come off the watermelon and will have to be cleaned out of the water.

Purpose or Benefit

"Greased Watermelon Polo" provides a good opportunity for physical exercise in the water.

High Water—Low Water

Number of Players:	4-12
Length of Time:	15-45 minutes
Material:	A rope at least eight feet long
Playing Site:	Large open area
Object of the Game:	To see how high one can jump without getting tangled in the rope.

To Play:

Two people are chosen to hold the ends of the rope and the rest of the players form a line. The rope holders begin by holding the rope taut and fairly close to the ground. One by one each person in line jumps over it.

The rope is then raised a little. The process is repeated until one person fails to clear the rope. Jumpers may *not* touch the rope with any part of their bodies. The person who misses then takes one end of the rope and the old rope holder gets in line to play the next round.

The next round starts with the rope close to the ground again.

Variation:

Instead of ending the round when one person misses, the play continues until only one person is left, and he is declared the winner.

Purpose or Benefit

"High Water—Low Water" presents a physical challenge, but is not "rowdy."

Hunker Hawser

Number of Players:	5-15
Length of Time:	10-30 minutes
Materials:	A long rope, at least 15 feet long, tied in a circle. Three or more pedestals (e.g., chairs, upended pails)
Playing Site:	Large open area with pedestals set up six feet apart, preferably on a soft surface such as grass or sand.
Object of the Game:	To be the last player standing on his pedestal.

To Play:

The pedestals are placed about six feet apart in a circle. The rope is placed around the circle allowing slack in between pedestals.

Each player mounts a pedestal and picks up the rope. The players can take any stance on the pedestals that helps them keep their balance.

At the starting signal, each player starts to pull on the rope, trying to unbalance the other players. The last player still on his pedestal is the winner.

Variation:

This game can be played on the ground using sturdy markers that players have to keep their feet on instead of using pedestals.

Purpose or Benefit

This game can help to develop strategy skills as well as balance.

Knots

Number of Players:	6-15
Length of Time:	10-60 minutes
Playing Site:	Large open area
Object of the Game:	To untie the knot of people.

To Play:

All the players stand in a circle, shoulder-to-shoulder, and join hands with two other players. No one should hold both hands of the the same person or join hands with the person next to him.

Now, everyone tries to untangle the knot and end up in a large circle. Pivoting hands, without breaking grip, is allowed (and encouraged) in order to avoid injury. The players may crawl over, under, and through one another in order to untie the knot.

Variation:

One player, called "Dr. Tangle," leaves the vicinity and does not observe what the other players do.

The others stand in a circle and join hands with the person on each side. Still holding hands, they walk in and out of the circle, over and under each other.

When they are sufficiently tangled they yell, "Help! Dr. Tangle!" Dr. Tangle comes to the rescue and directs the players in untangling themselves; it is *his* task to solve the puzzle. Their hands must remain held in their original order.

A new Dr. Tangle is chosen for each game.

Comments:

The knotted players will usually be untangled into one large circle, or occasionally into two small ones. Once in a while the tangle will be irresolvable without breaking hands. The Dr. Tangle variation is always resolvable.

This game is best played by groups of the same sex.

Purpose or Benefit

"Knots" and "Dr. Tangle" are physically active, challenging games that children especially enjoy.

Obstacle Course

Number of Players:	10-30
Length of Time:	1-2 hours
Materials:	Obstacles (i.e., buildings, furniture, tires, logs, bales, tennis balls, etc.) Blindfolds Paper bags
Playing Site:	This game is best played outdoors, al-

though the start and finish may be indoors.

Preparation:	Before the game begins, the obstacle course is established. Obstacle courses usually go around the perimeter of a building and are best when they include such obstacles as bushes, trees, sunken driveways, bales of straw or piles of logs, false walls, tennis balls in a closed area, or any other object which would confuse the blinded contestants.
Object of the Game:	To walk through the length of the obstacle course, blindfolded, from beginning to end.

To Play:

The group of players is divided into contestants and workers. There must be at least one worker for every contestant, although there can be more than one. Contestants are then blindfolded securely, and then bags are dropped over their heads as a double blind.

The game begins with the blinded contestants leaving the starting point. The contestants must travel the full length of the obstacle course blindfolded without touching one another or talking.

While the contestants are walking through the obstacle course, it is the workers' role to both protect them from serious harm and to harass them (for example, holding up a board in front of contestants in order to deceive them and make them believe they are encountering a wall so that they turn and walk in a wrong direction).

When the last contestant has completed the obstacle course, the game is finished.

Variations:

1. An obstacle course could be set up inside of a building.

2. Instead of harassing, the workers' purpose is to help the contestants go through the obstacle course, as in a "trust walk." One helper is assigned to each contestant. There

can also be workers who harass, but the helper protects the contestant or helps him recover from the harassment, giving the game obvious spiritual parallels.

Comments:

Discretion must be used in deciding how much the workers may harass the contestants. It is feasible, however, to allow workers to spin contestants in circles or even pull them off the trail.

Purpose or Benefit

This game could be played just to have fun, or it could be used to teach people the need for clear vision, both physically and spiritually. If the harassment is intense, the contestants will experience frustration and even anger because they will not know where they are going. This is also true for God's people when they don't have clear vision.

Prui (Proo-ee)

Number of Players: 10-100

Length of Time: 15-25 minutes

Playing Site: Large open area

Object of the Game: To find and become part of the Prui.

To Play:

Everyone stands in a group with eyes closed and starts moving around. One person acts as a referee to appoint the Prui and safeguard the other players.

The referee whispers to one person that he is the Prui. The Prui then opens his eyes. As people bump into each other they shake hands and ask, "Prui?" If the other person asks too, they know that neither of them is the Prui, because the Prui cannot talk.

If a player asks the question and gets no response, he opens his eyes and joins hands with the Prui, becoming part of it. The

Prui can be joined only at the ends, so if joined hands are found, the player has to follow the line to the end.

The referee appoints another Prui if the game is replayed.

Purpose or Benefit

"Prui" is good for all ages and can be played indoors or out, although the outdoor version may require a very attentive referee.

Red Rover, Red Rover

Number of Players: 10-30

Length of Time: 15-45 minutes

Playing Site: Outside in a large, grassy, open area

Object of the Game: To break through the other team's line and bring back their players.

To Play:

The players are divided into two teams, standing in lines a comfortable distance from each other for running.

One team begins by calling one person's name from the other team. "Red Rover, Red Rover, let (name) come over!" After they call "Red Rover . . . ," they hold hands tightly or lock arms.

The person whose name was called runs to the other team and tries to break through the line. If he succeeds, he returns to his team, bringing along a member of the opposing team to join them. If he fails, he joins the opposing team. The teams take turns calling "Red Rover, Red Rover. . . ."

The game ends when most or all of the players are on one team; that team wins.

Comments:

The roughness of the game tends to make it best for a group of older children.

Purpose or Benefit

"Red Rover, Red Rover" is an active, strenuous, and traditionally popular children's outdoor game.

Sardines

Number of Players:	5-15
Length of Time:	45-60 minutes
Playing Site:	A darkened house or outdoor area with places to hide
Object of the Game:	To find the person that is hiding, and those with him.

To Play:

Everyone is seated in one room that is closed off. One person is chosen to hide.

While everyone else remains in the closed room, the chosen person hides somewhere in the house. He needs about 5-8 minutes.

One person at a time (in four to five-minute intervals) goes out of the room, into the house to look for the hiding person. When he finds the hiding person, he *quietly* (it's hard) hides with him.

As each player comes to search, more and more players will be hiding together, like sardines, in one place or as close to it as possible.

The game ends when the last person finds where all the rest are hiding together.

The person who first discovered the original hider may start a new game as hider.

Comments:

"Sardines" is best played in a house that is unfamiliar to most of the players. Sardines is best with persons of the same sex, and is especially enjoyable for children.

Purpose or Benefit

"Sardines" brings a group close together. It promotes unity in a lighthearted way.

Simon Says

Number of Players:	3-30
Length of Time:	10-30 Minutes
Playing Site:	Adequate space for each player to move freely
Object of the Game:	To avoid being eliminated for acting out-of-turn.

To Play:

One player is appointed as "Simon." The other players situate themselves so that they can watch him and follow his directions.

Simon gives various commands, and demonstrates them himself as he does so. Common commands might be, "Simon says, 'Put your hands on your head,' " or "Simon says, 'Sit down.' "

Usually, Simon introduces his commands by saying, "Simon says." However, occasionally he does not, but says merely, "Put your hands on your head," for example.

The other players must obey Simon's commands *only* if he first says, "Simon says." If a player acts on a command not preceded by "Simon says," he is out of the game.

Play continues until all players except one have been eliminated. The only remaining player who has not acted out-of-turn wins. He may be appointed "Simon" for the next game.

Purpose or Benefit

"Simon Says" is a traditional children's game which encourages mental alertness and is also physically active.

Skin the Snake

Number of Players: 10-30

Length of Time: 10-20 minutes, depending on the number of players in each line

Playing Site: Large open area

Object of the Game: To lie down and stand up without breaking the chain.

To Play:

Players stand in several lines of 5 or more players each.

At a signal, each player bends forward slightly and puts his right hand through his legs. With his left hand, he grasps the right hand of the person in front of him. Thus, each line is a chain.

The person at the back of each line lies down (carefully), while the person in front of him walks backwards, straddling him. Each player successively lies down in the same way. The players must not let go of hands (break the chain). If they do so, they must start over.

When all the players on a team are lying down, the last person to lie down gets back up and walks forward, and the procedure is reversed.

The first team that has all lain down and stood up again without breaking the chain wins.

Comments:

"Skin the Snake" is best for children and groups of the same sex.

Purpose or Benefit

Team coordination is needed to successfully "skin the snake"; it is a unique and challenging race.

Water Slide

Number of Players:	2-20
Length of Time:	10-40 minutes
Materials:	A hose connected to a water source A long plastic sheet
Playing Site:	Large outdoor area that can stand getting very wet
Special Requirements:	Warm weather
Object of the Game:	To have a long, fun, wet, slide.

To Play:

The plastic sheet is laid on the ground and sprayed with plenty of water. Each player in turn takes a running slide.

Comments:

If played with children, care must be taken to have only one child on the slide at a time. Players should be warned ahead of time to dress for the game.

Purpose or Benefit

This is a great fun game to play on a very hot day.

Races and Relays

Balloon Relay

Number of Players:	10-30
Length of Time:	15-30 minutes, depending on the size of the teams
Materials:	2 balloons (have some spares in case these break)

Playing Site: Large open area

Object of the Game: To be first to get your team's balloon
                     to the goal and back.

To Play:

The players are divided into two groups and a goal is set up.

The players on each team go one-by-one to the goal, hopping on one foot and kicking the balloon with that foot. At the goal they switch the foot they are hopping and kicking with, and return. The team that gets all its players to the goal and back first wins.

Variation:

If children play this game, it is easier for them to use a broom instead of kicking.

Purpose or Benefit

This is a unique relay requiring coordination and providing excitement through team competition.

Can-Can Race

Number of Players: 2-30

Length of Time: 15-20 minutes

Materials: Enough large cans for 2 per player

Playing Site: Large open area

Preparation: Enough large cans need to be gathered. Large 46-ounce juice cans or #10 cans are best. The leader marks off starting and finish lines.

Object of the Game: To be the first to reach the finish line without falling off a can or touching the ground.

To Play:

All the players are lined up on the starting line. Each has one can on the ground/floor and another can in his hand. Each should have one foot on the can on the ground.

At the starting signal each player places his extra can on the ground in front of him and places his other foot on it. Then, without touching either foot to the ground, he bends over, picks up the first can, and moves it in front of him, placing his foot back on it.

He reaches back for the other can and repeats the process until one of the players successfully reaches the finish line, and wins the race.

If a player falls or touches the ground with any part of his body, he must pick up his cans and begin over from the starting line.

Variation:

This can be played as a relay race instead.

Comments:

It is good not to have a particularly long course as this is a difficult and exhausting race!

If adults and children compete together, children under 5 may have too difficult a time competing with older children and adults. They may need to be in a separate competition, paired with adults to help them hold their balance.

Purpose or Benefit

A fun, unusual game that can be played by all ages. A popular picnic game!

Cardboard Relay

Number of Players: 10-30

Length of Time: 15-45 minutes, depending on the size of the teams

Materials: 4 pieces of cardboard, about 10 inches square

Playing Site: Large open area

Object of the Game: To have all of your team go to the goal and return before the other team does.

To Play:

The players are divided into two teams. A goal is established for each team such that each team will have the same distance to travel to get to it. The teams stand in lines facing their respective goals. Each team is given two pieces of cardboard.

The first member of each team goes to his goal and back, walking on his pieces of cardboard. He does this by picking up a piece of cardboard with each step and placing it in front of the foot with which he is about to step.

When he returns to his team, the next person does the same thing, and in turn the rest of the team, until one team has had all its members go to the goal and return; that team wins.

Variation:

Instead of a relay race, each person can be given two pieces of cardboard, and a simultaneous race between all players can be conducted.

Comments:

This race is most successful when run on dry ground. If it is very wet, sturdy cardboard or plastic should be used.

Purpose or Benefit

Players are challenged to coordinate their feet and hands amidst the excitement of team competition.

Clothes Relay

Number of Players: 8-20

Length of Time: 20-40 minutes

Materials: 2 grocery sacks, each with a set of

large old clothes: a pair of pants, a shirt, a hat, pair of glasses and a necktie

Playing Site: Large open area

Object of the Game: To be the first team to have each person dress and undress.

To Play:

Players are divided into 2 equal teams. Each team forms a line. One sack of clothing is set at least 4 yards in front of each team.

The first player on each team runs to the sack of clothing, putting on each article of clothing in any order. Clothes need not be tied or buttoned.

Player then runs back to his team, tagging the next player in line. He runs back to the sack, takes off the articles and puts them back into the sack. He then runs to the next player in line and tags him again. The player goes to the end of the line and the second player takes his turn in the same fashion.

The game continues until all players of one team have had a turn, and thus win.

Variations:

1. After dressing, the player runs back to his team, takes clothes off and helps the next player get dressed.

2. The adult outfits can be more complicated, with suspenders to fasten, neckties to tie, etc.

If you don't have enough old clothes at home to use, some can be obtained inexpensively from places like the Salvation Army.

Purpose or Benefit

"Clothes Relay" is an active game for large groups. This is a popular picnic game and can be played by adults and children together or separately.

Drink-a-Cup

Number of Players:	5-20
Length of Time:	10 minutes
Materials:	A cup (paper or plastic) of water for each player
Playing Site:	Outdoors, or a spacious room that will not be damaged by water
Object of the Game:	To be the first to finish drinking a cup of water and return to the starting line.

To Play:

Players stand in a line. A finish line is designated. Each player is given a cup half-full of water. A nonparticipant serves as the referee.

When the referee gives a signal, players run, cup in hand, to the finish line. They kneel at the finish line, facing the starting line, and put their cups between their teeth and their hands behind their backs. They drink the water and then run back to the starting line. The first one to return to the starting line, wet or dry, wins.

Purpose or Benefit

Participants share the excitement of a race, and the amusement of attempting a task that all can do, but none can do perfectly.

Egg-Carry Relay

Number of Players:	8-100
Length of Time:	15-45 minutes
Materials:	A hard-boiled egg for each team A spoon for each team

Playing Site: Large open area

Object of the Game: To be the first team whose players all carry the egg across the goal line and back.

To Play:

The goal line is established. The players are divided into equal teams, each of which forms a line. The first player on each team is given a spoon with an egg balanced on it.

At a signal, the first player in each line carefully carries his egg to the goal line, then back to the second player in line. If the egg falls, the player must pick up the egg and go back to the starting line and begin again. The next player begins when the first player returns, and so on, until all the members of a team have completed the relay, and in so doing, win the game.

Variations:

1. Instead of walking, the players run or hop.

2. Split peas, fruits, or legumes are carried on a knife.

3. The knife may be carried in the player's mouth. In this case, each player should have his own knife.

4. Raw eggs prove to be more exciting.

Comments:

"Egg-Carry Relay" is a short game, usually played as one of a series of similar games.

Purpose or Benefit

Especially when repeated using different variations, this relay can be very amusing. It is an excellent game for picnics and other outdoor gatherings.

Flying Dutchman

Number of Players: 8-20

Length of Time: 15-45 minutes

Playing Site: Large open area

Object of the Game: To return to the hole in the circle be-
                       fore the opponents do.

To Play:

All but two players join hands and form a circle. The remaining two players are the lost ship and walk around the outside
of the circle looking for a "port." When they decide on a spot,
they break the handhold of any two players.

The lost ship must then travel around the circle one more
time. The two players who were broken apart must join hands
and run the opposite way around the circle trying to get back
to the "port" before the lost ship does. The first pair to arrive
closes the circle. The remaining pair is the new lost ship.

Variation:

For each game a rule could be made that players have to walk,
skip, hop, etc.

Purpose or Benefit

This game can easily be played by all ages as even very young
children can understand it.

Foul-Weather Relay

Number of Players: 8-40

Length of Time: 20-30 minutes

Materials: Two of each of the following:
                       Folding chairs
                       Umbrellas
                       Large pairs of overshoes or boots
                       Raincoats
                       Mittens
                       Hats

Playing Site: Large open area

Preparation: Players are divided into two teams,

standing in two single file lines. Two sets of props are placed approximately 10 feet in front of each team. The props are stacked in this order (bottom to top): 1 folding chair, 1 umbrella, 1 pair of overshoes, 1 raincoat, 1 hat, 1 pair of mittens.

Object of the Game: To be the team whose players complete the required actions first.

To Play:

A starting signal is given. The first player from each team runs forward to the props and puts the mittens on *first*. He puts the rest of the clothing on in *any* order, unfolds the chair and sits on it, and opens the umbrella *last*. The player must then reverse the order by closing the umbrella *first*, folding the chair, taking off the clothing in any order, and taking the mittens off *last*.

The player then runs back to his team and tags the next person who takes his turn, in the same way, and so on for the whole team. The first team whose players have finished wins.

Purpose or Benefit

"Foul-Weather Relay" is a hilarious game, and challenges the players' coordination.

Hobble Racing

Number of Players: 3-30

Length of Time: 10-20 minutes

Materials: A 3-foot piece of rope for each player

Playing Site: A 150-yard straight course is recommended

Preparation: Start and Finish lines are established.

Object of the Game: To cross the finish line first.

To Play:

Each player is given a rope with which he ties his knees together. At a signal he moves toward the finish line as quickly
as possible, by any means he can: waddling, hobbling, crawling, etc.

A player is disqualified if he purposely bumps another. The
first to cross the finish line wins.

Variation:

A "Three-Legged Race" can be run by forming teams of two.
Each team stands side-by-side and ties the two inside ankles
together. This forces team members to move their inside legs
as one.

Comments:

Three-Legged Race teams should decide before the race begins which legs will take the first step. Teams with players of
the same height will fare better than tall-short combinations.
Players may be allowed to practice their timing before the
race begins.

Purpose or Benefit

These races require discipline and concentration. The "Three-
Legged Race" promotes cooperation and unity between the
partners.

Islands

Number of Players:	10-30
Length of Time:	15-45 minutes
Materials:	Several Frisbees
Playing Site:	Large open area
Object of the Game:	To touch a Frisbee without touching anyone else.

To Play:

A few Frisbees are placed on the ground. One person acts as referee. The other players run around the area singing. When the leader says, "Islands!" everyone runs to touch a Frisbee. The last person to touch a Frisbee is out. Any two people that touch each other in the process of getting to the Frisbee are also out.

As people are eliminated, some of the Frisbees are removed until there is only one.

Purpose or Benefit

This game encourages quick thinking and speed with caution.

Knots and Blocks

Number of Players:	2-20
Length of Time:	10-45 minutes
Materials:	1 square wood block with a hole through it 1 8-foot piece of rope
Playing Site:	Large open area
Preparation:	The rope is threaded through the hole in the block. Knots are tied every 8-12 inches along the rope, with an equal number of knots on each side.
Object of the Game:	To reach the block first.

To Play:

A player stands at each end of the rope. At a signal, each player unties the knots until he reaches the block. Whoever reaches the block first pulls the block off the string and holds the prize as the winner.

Comments:

For more than two players, more than one rope and block can

be used, with all players simultaneously untying their knots and trying to reach their block first. Or, one rope and block is used for a series of contests. The winners of each contest play each other at the end.

Purpose or Benefit

Physical dexterity must be used competitively.

Monster Walk

Number of Players:	8-16
Length of Time:	10-20 minutes
Playing Site:	Large open area
Object of the Game:	To beat the opposing team over the finish line.

To Play:

Players are evenly divided into two teams. A starting line and a finish line about 10-20 yards apart are marked.

Each team forms a unit by joining hands, interlocking arms, riding piggy-back, or by any other means that can be devised. The only limitations are the number of arms and legs which may be used for the task of walking.

The number of arms and legs which can be used in the walking process are determined by subtracting two from the total number of people on the team. For example, if there are eight people on the team, six arms and six legs may be used.

To start the race, both teams assemble on the starting line. On signal, they move toward the finish line. The first team to arrive wins.

Purpose or Benefit

Success at "Monster Walk" requires interdependence and a unified effort.

Over and Under

Number of Players:	8-100
Length of Time:	15-30 minutes
Materials:	2 basketballs or 2 other large objects
Playing Site:	Large open area
Object of the Game:	To be the first team to complete the passing sequence.

To Play:

Players are divided into equal teams. Each team forms a line. The first player in each line is given a basketball.

At a starting signal, the first player in each line passes the basketball "over" his head to the second player, who then passes the ball "under" his legs to the third player in the line. The ball continues moving alternately "over and under" through the line of players until it reaches the last player.

The last player, upon receiving the ball, runs to the front of the line with the basketball and begins again by passing the ball "over" his head.

The game is continued in this manner until each person on the team has had his chance at the beginning of the line.

When the original first player on a team reaches the front of the line again, his team has won.

Purpose or Benefit

"Over and Under" is an exciting, fast-moving game that can include all ages.

Pickaback Relay

Number of Players:	10-20
Length of Time:	15-30 minutes

Playing Site:	Racecourse of 300-500 yards, wide enough for two runners
Object of the Game:	To be the first team to complete the course.

To Play:

The players are divided into two teams of equal size. Each team lines up behind the starting line and a rider is selected from each team, preferably a child.

The rider for each team begins on the back of its first runner, clasping his arms around the neck of the runner, and the runner hooks his arms under the rider's straddled legs.

At a starting signal the first runner of each team runs the course and returns to the starting line. The rider is then transferred to the back of the second runner without touching the ground, and the second runner then runs the course.

The process is repeated for all the members of the team. Dropping the rider while running the course does not disqualify the team.

The first team to have all its players run the course in this manner wins.

Variation:

For the adventurous, the racecourse could be made more interesting by the use of obstacles, such as running around trees, across streams, over low walls, etc.

Comments:

This is a physically demanding game; runners should be in good physical condition and strong enough to carry their riders.

Purpose or Benefit

"Pickaback Relay" provides an active physical game in which adults and children can participate together.

Potato-Sack Racing

Number of Players: 3-50

Length of Time: 10-20 minutes

Materials: Strong burlap sack for each partici-
                       pant

Playing Site: Large open area

Preparation: Clearly mark start and finish lines. If
                       children play, marking the track
                       along the way may help them find
                       their way more easily. It should be a
                       shorter distance for younger children.

Object of the Game: To be the first to cross the finish line.

To Play:

Each participant stands in a sack at the starting line, holding
the open edge. When signalled to start, all participants hop
toward the finish line. A judge at the finish line is helpful in
case of a close race.

A racer who purposely bumps into another racer to make him
fall is disqualified. A racer who falls may get up and continue.

Variations:

1. Players may race hopping backwards.

2. For larger groups the race may be done as a relay with
   players passing the gunny sack to the next player when
   they reach him.

Purpose or Benefit

"Potato-Sack Racing" is especially fun for children, or groups
of adults and children. It is a fun activity for picnics or other
gatherings on warm summer days.

Red Light—Green Light

Number of Players: 4-10

Length of Time: 15-45 minutes

Playing Site: Large open area

Object of the Game: To tag the "light" without being seen
                in motion.

To Play:

The player serving as the "traffic light" stands at one end of
the room. All the others stand at the other end.

Play begins when the light turns his back to the others and
says, "Green light." This is the signal for the others to advance toward the light.

At any moment, however, the light may turn around and say,
"Red light!" Everyone freezes as quickly as possible, because
anyone the light sees in motion must return to his starting
place.

The light alternates red and green until someone succeeds in
touching him without being seen, thus becoming the new
light.

Variation:

The light can also change by covering his face with a green pil-
low or other object for "green light" and removing it for "red
light."

Purpose or Benefit

Players learn to exercise self-control as they are held in suspense.

"Red Light—Green Light" can be used to help small children
learn colors and the meaning of traffic light signals.

Shoe Scramble

Number of Players:	8-30
Length of Time:	10-20 minutes
Playing Site:	Large open area
Object of the Game:	For each player to find his shoes from the pile and put them on.

To Play:

One player is the referee. All players take off their shoes and the referee mixes them all into a large pile in the center of the room. Players are divided into two teams and a captain is appointed for each team.

Each Team Captain decides relay order for the players on his team. At the referee's command, the first player on each team runs to the shoe pile, recovers his shoes, and puts them on. The shoes need not be tied.

The player then runs back to his team and tags the second player. The relay continues until all players on one team have recovered their shoes and put them on, thereby winning.

Variations:

1. All players on both teams recover their shoes all at once. The team whose players have all found their shoes first wins.

2. If there is a very large group, say over 30, the group can be divided into four teams instead of two. The first two teams go first, then the last two, then the winning teams from each round play each other.

3. Players must put their shoes on, with all buckles buckled, laces tied, etc.

4. If the game is played with teams mixed with adults and children, an adult or older child can be paired up with a younger child to help him find and put on his shoes. When played in pairs this way, younger children who are unable to tie or put on their own shoes are able to play.

5. To make the game easier the players remove only one shoe.

Purpose or Benefit

An active game for all ages, especially good for large group activities or picnics.

Soda Cracker Relay

Number of Players:	8-50
Length of Time:	15-20 Minutes
Materials:	2 soda crackers per player
Special Requirement:	Each player needs to be able to whistle
Object of the Game:	To be the team whose players all whistle after eating dry soda crackers.

To Play:

The players are divided into teams. Each player is given two soda crackers.

The first player on each team eats his crackers. As soon as he is able, he tries to whistle. When the first player of a team has whistled, the second player on that team may begin eating his crackers.

The game continues similarly with the rest of the team until the last person on one of the teams has whistled. The team that finishes first wins.

Variation:

The number of crackers each player must eat may be increased.

Purpose or Benefit

"Soda Cracker Relay" encourages teamwork and works well with a large group, yet it does not require as much space as most relays.

Spelling Relay

Number of Players:	10-30
Length of Time:	15-45 minutes
Materials:	Two complete sets of the alphabet on cards: letters on individual cards at least 4" x 5" (additional sets if group is very large)
Playing Site:	Large open area
Object of the Game:	To be the first team to spell the word.

To Play:

The group is divided into two or more teams. Each team stands in a line about 20 feet from a table or chair on which are a set of alphabet cards.

The leader prepares a list of words, preferably with no letter of the alphabet appearing more than once in each word.

The leader can limit his words to only certain letters if he wishes, or provide extra alphabet cards for letters he repeats in a word.

The leader tells how many letters are in the word he is about to pronounce and then says the word.

The first few players in each line (one player for every letter) run to their cards and arrange themselves facing their team, holding a card so that together they spell the word.

The first team to spell the word (correctly) receives a point; the leader keeps score. After each word, the players who tried to spell it go to the ends of their team lines.

The leader continues to call out words. If a word has the same letter more than once, he warns the players. They will have to wave the letter back and forth between the two positions where it appears in the word.

The team with the most points accumulated wins—at the end of the list of words, or at the leader's discretion.

Variations:

1. "Choose-and-Spell Relay": The leader calls out a category

rather than a word. Each team decides for itself what word it will spell that fits into the category. After they decide, the appropriate number of people run to the cards and spell the word. This variation requires creativity and increased teamwork.

2. "Spelling Backwards": The leader calls out a word, and the number of letters as in regular play. Each team must spell the word backwards.

Purpose or Benefit

"Spelling Relay" is enjoyable to children and adults and can provide good practice in spelling and working together as a team.

Spoon It Out

Number of Players:	4-12
Length of Time:	10-45 minutes
Materials:	2 blindfolds Cotton balls 2 large spoons 2 large bowls Clock or watch with a second hand
Playing Site:	Table and chair
Object of the Game:	To move the most cotton balls from one bowl into another.

To Play:

All the cotton balls are placed in one bowl. The full bowl and the empty bowl are placed side by side on the table.

A player is seated at the table, then blindfolded. He is allowed to feel where the bowls are in front of him *one* time. He must not touch the bowls or cotton balls with his hands at any point later on. Then he is given the spoon, and must try to move as many cotton balls as possible from the full bowl to the empty bowl, within a time limit. Each player takes a turn. The player who gets the most cotton balls into the empty bowl wins.

Variation:

"Spoon It Out" can be played as a relay. When one player is finished scooping, a teammate begins. The team which moves the most cotton balls from one bowl to the other wins.

Purpose or Benefit

"Spoon It Out" is as entertaining to *watch* as it is to play, and adapts itself well to any age group and time limitation.

Straws-and-Paper Relay

Number of Players:	6-30
Length of Time:	15 minutes
Materials:	One straw for each player 4 paper plates 4 chairs One 1/2" square paper for each player
Playing Site:	Large room
Object of the Game:	To be the first team whose players all have carried their paper squares to the empty paper plate.

To Play:

Players are divided into three teams, and each player is given a straw. Each team forms a line. A chair is placed 6-8 feet directly ahead of each team. A paper plate is placed on each of the three chairs, with a paper square for each player on the team placed on the paper plate. The fourth chair is placed directly in front of the teams—easily accessible by each. An empty paper plate is placed on the fourth chair.

On signal, the first player on each team walks forward to the chair in front of him with the straw in his mouth. He then sucks up a paper square with the straw and walks it back to the chair with the empty plate. If the square is dropped, it must be sucked up by the straw; no hands are allowed. When he reaches the empty plate he drops the square onto the plate, which then allows the second person to take his turn in like manner. The game continues until each player on one team has dropped his paper square onto the formerly empty paper plate. The team to complete this first wins.

Purpose or Benefit

"Straws-and-Paper Relay" can be very humorous, as players try not to laugh while having the straws in their mouths.

Tennis Ball Relay

Number of Players:	12-30
Length of Time:	10-20 minutes
Materials:	1 tennis ball for each player (all balls the same color)
Playing Site:	Large outdoor area, preferably grassy
Preparation:	The balls are marked sequentially up to the number of players there will be on each team, e.g., if each team will have six members, the balls will be marked "1," "2," "3," etc., through "6." A series of balls is marked for each team.
Object of the Game:	To retrieve and throw all the balls in numerical order before any other team does.

To Play:

Participants are divided into teams of equal size. A sequence of balls is tossed randomly but accessibly a short distance from each team.

When signalled to begin, the first player of each team finds its #1 ball, then runs back to his team and tosses the ball back into the field.

As soon as he has thrown it, the next player must retrieve the #2 ball, return, and toss it, and so on through the sequence. For large teams, it may be necessary to begin the sequence over again.

The first team to have retrieved and thrown all its balls, wins.

Purpose or Benefit

"Tennis Ball Relay" combines searching and throwing with the general excitement of a race.

Tag, Team Tag, and Capture Games

Blob Tag

Number of Players:	10-30
Length of Time:	15-45 minutes
Playing Site:	Large open area
Object of the Game:	To tag all the players, making them part of the Blob.

To Play:

The game starts as an ordinary game of tag except that as players are tagged, they join hands with "the Blob" (the person who is "it"), and thus become part of the Blob themselves. Only the outside hands of the Blob line can be used for tagging. The Blob can split itself, however, to catch stragglers.

The last person caught becomes the new Blob.

Comments:

Because the Blob can run only as fast as its slowest member, it is a good idea to try and tag the fastest runners first.

Purpose or Benefit

This is a good game for anyone who enjoys active games and it encourages working together as a body.

British Bulldog

Number of Players: 8-30

Length of Time: 15-30 minutes

Playing Site: Large open area

Object of the Game: To avoid being tackled. For the bulldog to tackle people.

To Play:

One person is selected to be the "bulldog." All other players
stand in a straight line side-to-side with arms extended to
touch the fingertips of the next person. This establishes the
width of the playing area. The length of the area should extend about 20 yards (to a finish line) from the line in which the
players are already standing (the starting line). These lines
are to be clearly identified.

The bulldog lies on his back in the center of the field of play.
When one player yells "Go," the bulldog gets off his back and
attempts to tackle one of the many players who are running en
masse toward the finish line.

Once a person is tackled, he becomes the bulldog's assistant.
In assuming this role, he joins the bulldog in tackling people
as they once again proceed from one line to the other.

As more people are tackled, more people become the bulldog's
assistants. This process continues until everyone has been
tackled. The last person tackled becomes the new bulldog.

Variation:

"Pom Pom": A less rambunctious version of "British Bulldog" replaces tackling with tagging. Also in "Pom Pom" the
person who is "it" begins the game standing rather than lying
on his back.

Comments:

It is recommended that this game be played at a fast pace in
order for it to be a valuable means of exercise.

Purpose or Benefit

"British Bulldog" is a popular boys' game and is a good tool
for developing appropriate boldness and courage.

Capture the Flag

Number of Players: 10-50

Length of Time: 45-90 minutes

Materials: Two makeshift flags

Playing Site: A large outdoor area with many potential hiding places.

Object of the Game: To capture the opposing team's flag and carry it to one's own side without being touched by an opponent.

To Play:

Players are divided into two equal teams. A central dividing line and encompassing boundaries are established. A captain may be appointed for each team.

Each team hides its flag in its own territory in such a way that the flag is clearly visible and reachable.

Each team chooses a "jailer" and an area to be the jail. Everyone else is assigned roles in accordance with the strategy of the team. Common roles include scouts, distractors, and territorial guards. These may be appointed by a captain who also leads the planning and execution of the team's strategy.

Each team, in accordance with its strategy, sends members into the opponents' territory in attempts to find and capture their flag.

If any player is captured (touched) by an opponent in the opposing team's territory, he must go to the jail of the opposing team. A jailed player can be set free by a member of his own team safely reaching the jail and touching him. Neither player is safe from being captured until he returns to his own territory.

When a person safely captures the other team's flag and brings it back to his own territory, his team wins.

Variations:

1. A neutral zone may be established between the territories of the opposing teams. Players are immune from capture while they are in this zone.

2. Players set free from jail may be given guaranteed safe return. In this case, however, they must return directly to their own territory and may not pick up their opponents' flag. The player who freed them should not be given guaranteed safe return.

Comments:

"Capture the Flag" is especially effective at dusk when visibility is decreased, but not so much so as to make running dangerous.

Purpose or Benefit

"Capture the Flag" is an exciting, active game which can involve cooperation and teamwork.

Dho-Dho-Dho

Number of Players:	10-30
Length of Time:	15-45 minutes
Playing Site:	Large open area with a surface soft enough to cushion falls (e.g., grass, beach, gym mat). The area is divided in half by a center line.
Object of the Game:	To capture all the players on the other team.

To Play:

The players are divided into two teams, standing on opposite sides of the dividing line. Each team chooses a player to be "it."

One "it" must run across the line, tag as many players as possible and return safely home. The tricky part is that "it" must do this all in one breath and he must repeat aloud, continuously, "Dho-dho-dho. . . ." If he gets back across the line with any part of his body, all those he tagged join his team.

The members of the opposite team may try to catch and hold

"it," above the waist, until he runs out of breath. If they succeed, "it" becomes part of their team. However, "it" cannot be caught until he touches someone first.

Teams alternate sending their "its" across the line until one side has all the players.

Variations:

1. Play the game for points rather than players.

2. Play the game as an elimination game with players going out instead of joining the opposite team.

Purpose or Benefit

This is an exciting game for large groups.

Duck, Duck, Goose

Number of Players:	5-25
Length of Time:	10-30 minutes
Playing Site:	Large open area
Object of the Game:	For "it" to tag a player.

To Play:

All players except "it" are seated in a circle on the floor (or ground). "It" walks around the outside of the circle tapping the head of each player he passes. With each tap he says either "duck" or "goose."

If he says "duck" no response is required by anyone. However, if "it" says "goose," the player being tapped tries to tag "it." "It" flees, running in one direction only around the circle until he reaches the spot formerly occupied by the pursuing player.

If "it" succeeds in sitting in the unoccupied spot without being tagged, the pursuer becomes the new "it," and play resumes as before. If, however, the pursuer tags "it," then "it" must sit in the middle of the circle until another player suffers the same lot.

When another player has been tagged, the newly tagged player must sit in the middle and the first one is freed to resume a seat as a part of the circle itself. The player who tagged "it" becomes the new "it," and again, play continues.

The game may continue until all have taken a turn as "it," or until the game has worn itself out.

Comments:

Usually, a limit is set on the number of times "it" may pass around the circle without saying "goose."

Purpose or Benefit

"Duck, Duck, Goose" is usually played by children. It is exciting and is easily learned.

Eeny-Einy-Over

Number of Players:	6-20
Length of Time:	20-60 minutes
Material:	Rubber gym ball
Playing Site:	Rectangular one-story house with a good yard for groups of people to run all the way around the house.
Object of the Game:	To capture all the members of the opposing team.

To Play:

One team has the ball and throws it over the house shouting "Eeny-einy-over!" The throwers then run clockwise around the house and try to tag as many members of the receiving team as possible.

Meanwhile, the receiving team must get the ball and run clockwise around the house to avoid being caught. They are considered free if they get around the first corner. If a person is tagged, he joins the other team.

If the ball does not make it over, there is no penalty. The throwers simply try again.

The play ends when all players are on the same team. Obviously, the only team remaining at the end of the game wins.

Variations:

1. The direction of running may be alternated between clockwise and counterclockwise.

2. Players are considered "free" only after they run all the way around the house and return back to their own side.

3. Players are considered "free" only after they run around the house and enter the opposing team's side.

Purpose or Benefit

"Eeny-Einy-Over" is a creative game of throwing and chasing.

English Fortress

Number of Players:	10-50
Length of Time:	15-45 minutes
Materials:	4 boundary markers
Playing Site:	Large open area, at least 50 feet wide and 70 feet long
Preparation:	Boundary markers are placed at the four corners of the playing area which define the sidelines and end lines of the field.
Object of the Game:	To capture all the members of the opposing team.

To Play:

The group is divided into two equal teams—a "Red" team and a "Blue" team, taking care to distribute fairly the slowest and fastest runners.

The teams go to opposite ends of the field and line up behind their respective end lines.

The Red team sends one member toward the Blue team. Each member of the Blue team remains behind the end line with one hand extended over the line. If any member of the Blue team crosses the end line without first being touched by the Red player, he must leave and join the Red team. This does not cause the round to end, however.

The Red player then touches the hand of one of the Blue team members and runs back toward his own team. If the Blue player tags the Red player before the Red player crosses his own team's end line, the Red player becomes part of the Blue team. If the Red player returns safely, the entire Red team chases the Blue player.

If one of the Red team touches the Blue player before the Blue player crosses his own end line, he becomes a member of the Red team. If the Blue player returns safely, the entire Blue team pursues the entire Red team.

When all the members of the Red team have either crossed their own end line or have been captured, the round is completed.

Once the teams are realigned, the procedure is repeated with a member of the Blue team opening the round. This alternation continues until all the members of one team have been captured.

A round ends immediately when a player has been captured. The only exception to this occurs when an entire team is being pursued. In this case, the round does not end until every player of the team being chased has either reached safety or has been captured. A round is likely to end before reaching this point.

Purpose or Benefit

"English Fortress" is suitable for adults and children. It is exciting, energetic, and gets every participant actively involved.

Flashlight Tag

Number of Players:	5-15
Length of Time:	15-45 minutes
Material:	Flashlight
Playing Site:	Large open outdoor area Complete darkness
Object of the Game:	To tag "it" without first being spotted with the flashlight.

To Play:

The person who is "it" has the flashlight. Boundaries are established at a radius of approximately 50 yards from "it."

Players are given a brief period to run anywhere within the boundaries before "it" can use his flashlight. When that period is over, "it" tries to "tag" people by spotting them with his flashlight before they can sneak back and touch him.

Once a person has been spotted with the flashlight he is eliminated.

Comments:

Players may strategize together to distract "it" and sneak up on him.

Purpose or Benefit

Players have an opportunity to exercise caution, perceptiveness, self-control, and teamwork.

Fox and Geese

Number of Players:	3-12
Length of Time:	10-45 minutes
Playing Site:	A spacious blanket of undisturbed snow

Preparation: A wheel-shaped design is made in the snow by walking on it. The diameter of the wheel and the number of spokes varies with the number of people playing and the area of snow available.

Object of the Game: To catch a goose or avoid being caught by the fox.

To Play:

One player is the "fox" and all the others are the "geese" he tries to catch. During the chase, all players must stay on the paths made in the snow.

Certain spots on the wheel are designated as "safe" for the geese, i.e., a goose is immune from being tagged by the fox while on a spot. However, if another goose comes, the goose on the spot must relinquish his position to the new goose. The safety spots are usually at the center of the circle and/or at intersections of the spokes and the rim. The center of the circle makes the best safety spot.

The first goose caught by the fox becomes the new fox.

Variation:

Players may wish to experiment with other designs for paths, such as a figure eight or a four-leaf clover.

Purpose or Benefit

Playing "Fox and Geese" is an excellent way to get fresh air and exercise in the winter.

Fox in a Tree

Number of Players: 10-20

Length of Time: 15-45 minutes

Playing Site: Large open area

Object of the Game: For the hound to catch a fox, for the foxes to not get caught by the hound.

To Play:

Players are grouped into circles of 4-6 persons. One person in each circle is the "fox." The players hold hands, with the fox protected in the center. There are two stray players not in a circle, one is a fox and the other is a hound. The hound begins to chase the fox around the room; yard.

The fox may take refuge in a "tree" (a circle of players). When the fox enters a tree, the previous fox hiding in that tree must leave and be chased by the hound. When the hound catches a fox, that fox becomes the hound and the hound becomes the fox.

Variation:

For a larger group, there can be 2 hounds chasing 2 stray foxes outside of the trees/circles. Played in this way, the game can be played with up to 30 players.

Comments:

Time should be allowed to regroup a few times so that each player has a chance to be a fox or a hound.

Purpose or Benefit

"Fox in a Tree" is an active game which is easier to play for some children than the standard "tag."

Go-Tag

Number of Players:	6-20
Length of Time:	15-45 minutes
Playing Site:	Large open area
Object of the Game:	The chaser tries to tag the runner.

To Play:

All players squat in a row with alternate players facing opposite directions.

The person at one end of the row becomes the first runner. He may go either direction around the row. The person at the other end is the chaser. The chaser may start in either direction, but may not change directions once started.

As the chaser goes around the track, he may tag any player on the back and shout, "Go!" The tagged player then becomes the new chaser and the chaser replaces him squatting in line.

The key to the game is to change chasers often, keeping the runner off guard.

When the runner is tagged, he squats at one end of the line, and the person who tagged him becomes the new runner. The person at the other end of the line becomes the new chaser.

Purpose or Benefit

"Go-Tag" incorporates teamwork and strategy and provides good exercise.

Hope to See the Ghost Tonight

Number of Players: 6-20

Length of Time: 30-45 minutes

Playing Site: Large open area

Special Requirement: Best played in the dark

Object of the Game: For the Ghost to catch everyone else.

To Play:

One player is designated as the "Ghost." The Ghost is then given several minutes to hide within the set boundaries of the game area.

After the Ghost has hidden, the remaining players begin wandering around the game area, each walking by himself. As they walk, players repeat the sentence, "I hope to see the Ghost tonight."

When a player passes by the spot where the Ghost is hiding, the Ghost jumps out and tags him. The player who was caught then hides with the Ghost, becoming a Ghost himself. When the next player passes by the hiding spot, both Ghosts catch him. This continues until all players have been caught.

Comments:

The larger the group, the more exciting this game is.

Purpose or Benefit

"Hope to See the Ghost Tonight" is an easy game with the added excitement of suspense in a darkened playing area. It is a good game for a group of mixed ages to play.

Kick the Can

Number of Players:	5-10
Length of Time:	30-60 minutes
Material:	A large empty can
Playing Site:	Large open area
Object of the game:	Boundaries are set for hiding places and a site to be the goal is selected.

To Play:

The players choose one person to be "it," and position him and the can at the goal. All the other players hide.

After all the others hide, the person who is "it" tries to find them. Whenever he finds someone, he says his name. The person found is "caught" and must go to the goal. Any of the players who are hiding can go to the goal and kick over the can, which frees all who have been caught to hide again. The person who is "it" cannot catch someone who is obviously on the way to kick the can. The game ends when the person who is "it" finds everyone without the can being kicked over.

Comments:

It is best not to play with too large a group, or else "it" will be "it" forever. If this situation arises, the group may change the rules to make it easier for "it," select a new "it" after a certain time span, or have two "its."

Purpose or Benefit

"Kick the Can" is an active, exciting game which requires ingenious thinking on the part of all players.

Link Tag

Number of Players: 10-30

Length of Time: 15-45 minutes

Playing Site: Large open area

Object of the Game: For "it" to catch the runner; for the runner to evade "it" by joining a pair.

To Play:

The group decides who will be "it." The rest of the players form pairs. An extra person may join a pair to form a threesome. Each pair chooses a place to stand, and links arms.

One of the players is chosen to be the runner, who tries to link up with one of the pairs without being caught by "it." If he is caught, he becomes "it." If he links up with one person of a pair, the person on the other end becomes the runner, and runs to another pair trying not to get caught.

Comments:

Much confusion will be avoided if players make sure that they are not leaving their pairs and running until the runner has actually linked up with another player (not merely touching another's arm).

Purpose or Benefit

The running required in "Link Tag" is good exercise, and the element of pursuit provides excitement. This form of tag is easier for persons who are not fast runners because they have opportunities to "get safe" and rest by linking up with a pair.

Mariner

Number of Players:	8-24
Time Needed:	15-60 minutes
Materials:	A blindfold for each player Wrestling mats (if playing indoors) Rope, or a shovel to dig a trench (if playing outside)
Playing Site:	Large, open area
Preparation:	Boundaries that can be felt are set up in a 15-yard square. These dimensions can be freely altered to accommodate the size of the group or one's preference.
Object of the Game:	To tackle and pin the opponents until all are eliminated from the game.

To Play:

One person is designated to be the referee. The remainder of the participants are divided into two equal teams. Each team devises a secret code that can be used by the teammates to identify one another.

All players are blindfolded. On signal from the referee, everyone begins to grope around within the boundaries until he finds another player. When this happens, both players attempt to determine by use of their prearranged code whether the other person is on the same team or not. If they are on the same team, both players part and continue groping in order to encounter other players. If they discern, however, that they belong to different teams, each of them attempts to tackle the other person, force him onto his back, and hold him in this position. If a person is contained in this position for three seconds, the player on top yells, "Mariner!"

At this point, all action stops. The blindfolds of the two players involved are removed and the referee decides if the person was pinned adequately. If not, both players put their blindfolds back on and return to the game after being disoriented (spun around) by the referee.

If the pin was satisfactory, the player who was pinned leaves the game while the other returns after being disoriented. This procedure continues until only members of the same team remain.

If a player tackles a member of his own team, the person tackling is eliminated from the game.

Variation:

The playing area can be divided into halves, thus giving each team a respective "home" and "away" court. In this version players must be in their "away" court in order to be tackled.

Comments:

Pinning a player means that one person simply holds another person's back to the floor. This differs from a pin in wrestling which requires that both shoulder blades be held tightly to the ground.

Purpose or Benefit

Playing "Mariner" develops strength, boldness and courage in its participants. It is a popular boys' game.

Prisoner's Base

Number of Players:	20-30
Length of Time:	20-60 minutes
Materials:	Bandanas, handkerchiefs, or other identifying devices for half the players
Playing Site:	Large open area
Preparation:	A 30-60-foot square field is marked with a center line: A 2-foot diameter circle is marked in the middle of the center line. This circle is the "chivy." In the corners of the field a prison and a home base are designated for each team. They are arranged so that the

two prisons are kitty-corner across from each other and likewise the home bases.

Object of the Game: To capture all members of the opposing team.

To Play:

Choose two teams of equal size. One team wears a distinguishing mark, such as a bandana tied around the arm.

All players are situated in their respective home bases. A captain is selected for each team. The team that starts is determined by a coin toss or similar method.

The captain of the starting team sends a runner to the chivy. When the runner arrives there, he says, "Chivy!" This cues the opposing captain to send a runner to tag him. Then the starting captain sends a runner to tag the opposing runner. This process continues until every player is attempting to tag another.

Players are safe only at their respective home bases. When a player is tagged by an opponent he must remain in the opposing team's prison until a teammate frees him by tagging him.

The team who manages to keep all opponents in prison at one time wins. However, often the game is ended by common assent when the players are too exhausted to continue.

Comments:

"Prisoner's Base" can continue for long periods of time and easily reaches riotous conditions.

Purpose or Benefit

Vigorous physical activity is combined with teamwork and cat-and-mouse excitement.

Rattlers

Number of Players: 8-20

Length of Time: 15-45 minutes

Materials: 2 blindfolds
2 rattles, which can be made of cans and pebbles

Playing Site: Large open area

Object of the Game: For the chaser to tag the other rattler.

To Play:

Two players are chosen as rattlers. The others form a circle around them, forming the "snake pit." Each rattler is blindfolded and given a rattle. One rattler is chosen as the chaser, the other is the quarry.

If one of the rattlers wants to find out where the other one is, he shakes his rattle. The other rattler must respond by shaking his. The *chaser* is allowed to initiate *only five shakes*, but the quarry can shake as much as he wants to.

The other players keep the rattlers in the snake pit and cheer them on. It is also helpful if they count the chaser's shakes. They may move around to change the shape of the snake pit at any time during the game.

When the chaser finally catches his prey, two new rattlers are chosen, or one or both of the rattlers may take the opposite role, filling any vacant role with a player from the circle.

Purpose or Benefit

Besides the excitement of a chase, players also experience the challenge of depending on senses other than sight.

Rock, Paper, Scissors Tag

Number of Players: 10-30

Length of Time: 15-45 minutes

Playing Site: A large open area divided by a center line. There is a "free zone" at the far end of each half; the boundary lines designating the free zones are parallel to the center line.

Object of the Game: To beat the opposite team in showing the symbol and catching their players.

To Play:

This game is based on the old Rock, Paper, Scissors game.

An open, flat hand is the symbol for Paper. A fist symbolizes Rock, and two extended fingers represents Scissors.

The order of strength is: paper covers rock; rock breaks scissors; scissors cut paper.

The players are divided into two teams. The teams huddle and decide which signal they will show. They should have a second choice in case both teams give the same symbol.

The teams then line up on either side of the center line and chant, "Rock-Paper-Scissors." On the next beat each team shows its symbol.

The winning team then tries to tag as many of their opponents as possible before the opponents reach their free zone.

Those tagged are either eliminated from the game or join the opposing team. The game continues until there is only one team.

Purpose or Benefit

This is a good game for all ages and lots of players. It encourages team work and cooperation as well as a quick eye and lightning responses.

The Sea Is Rough

Number of Players: 6-20

Length of Time: 15-45 minutes

Playing Site: Large open area

Object of the Game: To be the last person caught by the sea.

To Play:

One player is "the sea." Each of the other players identifies himself as a different sea creature. Each sea creature finds a spot where he will stand at the beginning of the game and will try to get back to it at the end of the game.

The sea marches, runs, skips, etc., past each player. As he calls their names (sea creatures), they follow and imitate him.

The sea then gets faster and "rougher," winding in circles, etc., and eventually yells, "The sea is rough!"

The sea creatures must find their original spots while the sea tries to catch them. Any creature the sea touches before it gets back to its original spot becomes part of the sea, and assists in following-the-leader and chasing creatures until everyone becomes part of the sea. The last creature caught is the winner.

Purpose or Benefit

"The Sea Is Rough" is a creative form of tag which can be played by groups of children and/or adults.

Shepherd and Wolf

Number of Players:	6-30
Length of Time:	20-90 minutes
Playing Site:	Large open area
Object of the Game:	For the sheep to reach the shepherd without being captured by the wolf.

To Play:

The leader of the game designates one player to be the "shepherd" and another to be the "wolf." The remaining players are "sheep." If the group is large (perhaps over 15), more than one wolf and shepherd may be chosen.

The sheep all line up at one end of the field or room. The shepherd is at the other end, with the wolf between them. The shepherd calls his sheep, two or three at a time. They try to reach him without being caught by the wolf. When a sheep is caught by the wolf, he is taken to the wolf's "den," a designated portion of the field or room, such as a tree or a corner.

The shepherd may go to the den and rescue the sheep only when the wolf is not there, and the wolf may go to the shepherd's fold to capture sheep only when the shepherd is not there.

When the last stray sheep is either caught by the wolf or reaches the shepherd, the number of sheep each has is totalled. If the wolf has a greater number than the shepherd, he becomes the shepherd. If not, he may remain as the wolf the second time the game is played, or choose one of the sheep he has caught to be the wolf.

Purpose or Benefit

"Shepherd and Wolf" is exciting, active, and especially enjoyable for children.

Smaug's Jewels

Number of Players:	6-20
Length of Time:	15-45 minutes
Material:	Handkerchief or similar item to serve as Smaug's jewels
Playing Site:	Large open area
Object of the Game:	To capture Smaug's jewels without being tagged.

To Play:

One person is picked to be "Smaug," the dragon. His jewels (a handkerchief or similar item) are placed on the ground beside him. The other players stand around Smaug and try to snatch the jewels.

A person touched by the mighty Smaug is frozen in place for the duration of the dragon's reign. The dragon may roam as far from the treasure as he wishes.

When a player captures the treasure, he becomes the new Smaug.

If Smaug somehow manages to freeze everyone without some- one snatching the jewels, he has the option of leaving everyone frozen solid for 300 years. Christian dragons rarely do this; usually they appoint a new player to be Smaug.

Comments:

This game's title is based on the dragon, Smaug, from Tol- kien's novel, *The Hobbit*.

Purpose or Benefit

"Smaug's Jewels" is very adaptable to indoor and outdoor set- tings and can be played easily by all ages. It encourages strat- egy and cooperation.

Wells Fargo

Number of Players:	10-30
Length of Time:	1-2 hours
Materials:	2 blocks of wood for each team— about 8"x2"x1" Colored tape—different color for each team Hoop, inner tube, or rope
Playing Site:	Large outdoor area with plenty of places in which to hide
Special Requirement:	Participants should wear old cloth- ing, as it may get dirty or torn.
Object of the Game:	To deliver as much gold as possible to the bank and to steal the opponents' tape.

To Play:

Participants are divided into teams of equal size. Each team has a different color of tape stuck to the foreheads of its members. Two blocks of wood are given to each team as its "gold."

A hoop or similar object is identified as the bank and is centrally located.

A referee keeps track of points scored by each team.

Before actual play begins, each team must confer to plan a strategy, appoint two teammates as its gold carriers, and then scatter and hide. The referee should allow about 10 minutes for these preliminaries. When the referee declares time-in, all players should be hiding, with the gold carriers holding the gold.

When the action begins, players attempt to remove the tape from their opponents' foreheads and to steal their gold. They also attempt to deliver as much gold as possible, stolen or otherwise, to the bank.

In order to steal gold, they must remove the tape from the foreheads of opposing gold carriers. A carrier who is de-taped must surrender his gold to his attacker. The gold robber then tries to deliver his loot to the bank before *he* is robbed. Any player, gold carrier or not, whose tape is removed is out of the game, and remains in the bank area until the game is over.

Strategy may include hiding, guarding the gold carriers or the bank, sneaking around, chasing, dodging, or seeking out the opposing gold carriers, etc.

Teammates may not pass the gold among themselves. It remains with a given gold carrier until it is stolen, delivered to the bank, or stolen back.

A player may not remove his own tape to replace it at a later point in the game. The penalty for so doing is to leave the game and surrender his tape to his opponents.

The game ends when all the gold has been delivered to the bank. Points are scored as follows:

Each block of a team's own gold delivered	= 20
Each block of stolen gold delivered	= 50
Each piece of tape unremoved from a team member's forehead	= 10
Each piece of stolen tape	= 10

The team with the most points is the winner.

Variation:

Tape is placed on players' backs instead of on their foreheads. Pieces of colored cloth can also be used, tucked into back pockets or waistbands, partially exposed.

Purpose or Benefit

"Wells Fargo" is rough and exciting, but not dangerous. It is a good active game for a long summer day.

Traditional Sports with a Twist

Backwards Nerf Ball

Number of Players:	10-20
Length of Time:	30-90 minutes
Materials:	Plastic baseball bat Ball (Nerf or other)
Playing Site:	Baseball diamond
Object of the Game:	To score the most runs.

To Play:

"Backwards Nerf Ball" is played like baseball or softball, only after hitting the ball, the runner must run backwards around the bases and the fielders must run backwards to field the ball.

Purpose or Benefit

"Backwards Nerf Ball" provides physical exercise and much laughter. This game is fun to play with adults and children together.

Broom Hockey

Number of Players:	16-40
Length of Time:	30-60 minutes
Materials:	2 chairs 2 brooms The puck: 1 large rag, tied in a big knot if played indoors; a small ball if played outdoors.
Playing Site:	Large open area
Preparation:	Players are divided into two teams, in rows facing each other, about 10 feet apart. A chair is placed at each end of the rows, halfway between the two rows. The puck is placed in the center of the field. The chairs are identified as the respective team goals.
Object of the Game:	To hit the puck under the chair (goal) with a broom more times than the other team.

To Play:

The player at the end of one line and the player at the opposite end of the other line are each given a broom. At a signal they both enter the field and hit the puck with their brooms, trying to knock it through their respective goals. When one of them succeeds, his team scores a point.

The brooms are passed to each successive person in the team lines until all have had a turn. The team with the most points wins.

Comments:

"Broom Hockey" is usually played in stocking feet when played indoors.

A wise game organizer will make sure that each pair of players who will be on the field at the same time is fairly evenly matched in skill.

Purpose or Benefit

"Broom Hockey" incorporates a large number of people and is good for teenagers and young adults.

Commando Basketball

Number of Players:	12-20
Length of Time:	30-90 minutes
Material:	One basketball
Playing Site:	Basketball court
Preparation:	A "commando drill" (which should last no more than one minute) is determined. Such a drill is composed of a combination of exercises (e.g., running two laps around the court, doing ten push-ups and ten sit-ups).
Object of the Game:	To be the team that makes the most baskets.

To Play:

"Commando Basketball" is like conventional basketball with the following variations:

1. No fouls are called.

2. Double-dribble and traveling are illegal and punishable by the commando drill.

3. If a man scores a basket, the player guarding him must perform the commando drill.

4. When a person leaves the game to do a commando drill, another player replaces him. The player leaving the game goes to the end of the "substitute line," which consists of players waiting for their turn to enter the game.

Variation:

This game may also be played without substitutes. When a player leaves the game to go through his commando drill, his team simply plays without him.

Purpose or Benefit

"Commando Basketball" is especially useful for developing perseverance and physical endurance.

Floor Hockey

Number of Players:	6-20
Length of Time:	20-90 minutes
Materials:	1 plastic hockey stick for each player 1 plastic puck 4 stationary objects (which form the goals)
Playing Site:	A large uncarpeted surface
Preparation:	Two stationary objects are taken to each end of the floor and positioned three feet apart halfway between the side lines. These make up the goals.
Object of the Game:	To score more goals than the opposing team.

To Play:

The players are divided into two teams of equal size.

At the start of the game, all players assume their positions. If there are six players on a team, there will be one stationed at the center of the court, one goalie, two on either side of the goal being defended, and two players on either side of the goal in which they hope to score. If teams are comprised of more or less than six players each, adaptations can be made to this arrangement of positions.

Play begins when the two players at the center have the puck placed between them and, after they tap each other's sticks three times, they both begin to strike the puck so as to move it toward the goal in which they hope to score. Other players become involved in the action as the puck moves into other regions of the court. Each player's intent is to hit the puck toward his own goal and to prevent the opposing team from scoring.

The following actions are illegal and result in removal from the game for 90 seconds:

1. Swinging the blade of a stick above waist level.

2. Using the hands or elbows for hitting, shoving, etc.

The team ahead at the end of the time allotted wins.

Comments:

This game does allow physical contact and roughness (such as ramming into an opponent) and is not recommended for the faint-hearted.

Purpose or Benefit

"Floor Hockey" encourages participants to conduct themselves in boldness and courage. Teamwork can also be trained and developed.

Frisbee Football

Number of Players:	6-20
Length of Time:	45-90 minutes
Materials:	One Frisbee White lime, string, or some other means of marking a field
Playing Site:	Large open outdoor area
Preparation:	Mark the approximate dimensions of a football field in the playing area. Three lines are also marked across the field—one at midfield and the others halfway between the midfield line and the goal lines.
Object of the Game:	To cross the goal line with possession of the Frisbee.

To Play:

"Frisbee Football" is played like touch football with the following differences:

1. The team "kicking off" throws the Frisbee from its own goal line.

2. A first down is gained when a team crosses the midfield line with the Frisbee or when three consecutive forward passes are completed in one series of downs.

3. Like kick-offs, punts are thrown. If the Frisbee goes beyond the end zone on either punts or kick-offs, it is returned to the nearest quarter-field line. If it goes out of bounds on a punt or kick-off, the receiving team has the choice of moving the line of scrimmage either to midfield or to the place where the Frisbee went out-of-bounds.

Variation:

"Frisbee Football" can be played like tackle football rather than touch.

Purpose or Benefit

"Frisbee Football" provides a good opportunity for physical exercise and teamwork.

Frisbee Golf

Number of Players:	2-6
Length of Time:	30-90 minutes
Materials:	One Frisbee for each player
Playing Site:	A large outdoor area, preferably a large park or similar area
Preparation:	The game planner may lay out a golf course before the game, or it can be laid out one target at a time. For each pin (known also as hole or target), an object is chosen (e.g., a tree, can, sprinkler).
Object of the Game:	To get your Frisbee to each of the pins in the least number of throws.

To Play:

Each player attempts to throw his Frisbee to the first pin.

Each player's score is the number of throws he has taken.

Players move from pin to pin until the entire course has been played. Rules follow normal golf rules. Frisbees are thrown from where they land.

If a well-meaning passer-by throws a Frisbee back to a player, the player must throw it from where it lands, unless the player catches it, in which case, the player throws again and deducts one point.

Comments:

If there are more than six players, they can play in pairs or foursomes as in golf.

Purpose or Benefit

This is a good outdoor game that needs little equipment. It is a fun way to play Frisbee and a unique way to play golf!

Frisbee Keep-Away Tag

Number of Players: 6-20

Length of Time: 15-45 minutes

Material: Frisbee

Playing Site: Large open area

Object of the Game: To keep the Frisbee away from those who are "it."

To Play:

Boundaries are determined, allowing plenty of room to run.

Between one-third and one-half of the players are designated as "it."

When the game commences, the Frisbee is thrown from player to player, with hopes of keeping it away from the players who are "it." If a player who is "it" gains possession of the Frisbee, the person who last threw the Frisbee is now "it," and the person securing the Frisbee is now no longer "it."

If a player who is "it" tags a player holding a Frisbee, they exchange positions.

If a player throws a Frisbee out-of-bounds, he becomes "it." The only players eligible to retrieve the Frisbee are the other players who are "it." The one who gains control of the Frisbee is no longer "it."

Variation:

"Frisbee Keep-Away Tag" can be played in a lake or a pool. If played in a lake, buoys may be used to define boundaries.

Purpose or Benefit

Playing "Frisbee Keep-Away Tag" wholeheartedly furnishes an excellent exercise activity. It is also a fun way for a large group of people to play Frisbee together.

New Frisbee

Number of Players:	2-12
Length of Time:	10-60 minutes
Material:	Frisbee
Playing Site:	Large open area
Object of the Game:	To score points and improve skill in throwing and catching a Frisbee.

To Play:

Each player announces which hand he will use to throw and catch. One hand may be used to catch and the other to throw but they must stay the same during the game. The player who catches decides the points for both himself and the thrower.

Scoring: If the catcher gives his all to make a catch and still misses it, he gives himself one point. If the throw is direct and easy and the catcher misses it, the thrower gets a point.

If both the throw and catch are good, no points are scored.

If the catcher fumbles and drops the Frisbee, the thrower gets two points.

If the Frisbee tilts more than 45 degrees from horizontal during flight the catcher yells "forty-five" and gives himself a point.

Any other scoring may be decided by the players.

The Frisbee is thrown from one player to another in rotation so that each player has the same number of turns.

Purpose or Benefit

Good exercise is provided for all and Frisbee skills are improved in "New Frisbee."

Ultimate Frisbee

Number of Players:	6-24
Length of Time:	20 minutes-2 hours
Material:	Frisbee
Playing Site:	A large, open field
Preparation:	Clearly marked boundaries should enclose a playing area approximately the size of a football field. Goals for each team are established.
Object of the Game:	To score the most goals by advancing the Frisbee upfield.

To Play:

"Ultimate Frisbee" is similar to football, but it has unique qualities. Once teams have been equally divided, a toss of the coin decides which team receives and which "throws off."

At the outset of the game, the team "throwing off" (comparable to kicking off in football) lines up at midfield to throw the Frisbee to the opposing team. Once this happens, the action is continuous until either a goal is scored or the Frisbee goes out-of-bounds.

Players then work to advance the Frisbee toward their goals

by passing it down the field. Players are not allowed to run while carrying the Frisbee. The only way the Frisbee can be moved is by throwing it. If a player who is chasing the Frisbee catches it, he is allowed to take no more than three steps after the reception.

A goal is scored when a player has secure possession of the Frisbee beyond the proper goal line.

When the Frisbee goes out-of-bounds, it is given to the team which did *not* touch it last. Resume play by throwing the Frisbee in from the point where it went out-of-bounds.

Players are not allowed to block, tackle or otherwise physically interfere with other players.

The team not in possession of the Frisbee should focus its efforts on intercepting or blocking passes in order to gain control for themselves.

The team scoring the most goals at the end of a predetermined period of time (e.g., 30 minutes) is the winner.

Variation:

The "commando" version allows for tackling, blocking, and other forms of bodily contact.

Comments:

The "commando" version tends to be rough, sometimes damaging the Frisbee (and the players).

Purpose or Benefit

"Ultimate Frisbee" provides an excellent opportunity for vigorous exercise. Teamwork and endurance are required for success.

New Volleyball Variations

Number of Players: 12-30

Length of Time: 20-90 minutes

Materials: Volleyball and net

Playing Site: Normal volleyball court

Object of the Game: To score the most points as a team by
                         returning the ball over the net.

To Play:

Standard volleyball rules are followed with the following variations:

1. Rotation ball: Instead of rotating players within each team, they are rotated to the other team after both have served.

2. Volley-volley ball: Points are scored by the number of times a team hits the ball before getting it over the net. Thus a team can get from one to three points at a time. A game is 35 points.

3. Volley-volley-volley ball: Two energetic teams might try using the rule that every member of the team must hit the ball at least once before it is returned. This works best with fewer players. A game is nine points.

4. Infinity ball: The score is the number of times the ball goes over the net before it touches the ground. A score over 50 is good and both teams win!

5. Badminton: Any of the above variations are played except with badminton racquets and birdies.

Purpose or Benefit

These variations encourage cooperation rather than competition.

Round Robin

Number of Players: 6-30

Length of Time: 10-60 minutes

Materials:	Table tennis table and net
	Table tennis ball(s)
	2 table tennis paddles

Object of the Game: To consistently return the ball.

To Play:

Half of the players stand in a line beginning at the middle on one end of the table and extending to the left of the first player, who is facing the table. The rest of the players are arranged similarly at the other end of the table.

The player at the beginning of one of the lines serves the ball, then places his paddle on the table and proceeds to the end of the line at the opposite end of the table. The player at the beginning of the other line returns the ball, sets his paddle down, and likewise gets in line.

By the time the ball has been served and returned, the second player in the server's line has picked up the paddle to continue the volley. The play continues in this way, each player hitting the ball once and immediately getting ready for his next turn, at the opposite end.

If a player fails to serve or return the ball legally (according to normal table tennis rules), he has a violation. Players may determine before they begin play how many violations a player is allowed before he is eliminated from the game.

When all players except two have been eliminated, the two remaining must place their paddles on the table and spin around after each time they hit the ball.

The last player remaining is the winner.

Purpose or Benefit

"Round Robin" is fast-moving and energetic. Skill is helpful but not necessary to play and enjoy the game. It is a good way for a large group of people to play ping-pong together.

Siamese Soccer

Number of Players:	16-30
Length of Time:	30-60 minutes
Materials:	Three-foot length of rope for each pair of players Soccer ball Soccer goals
Playing Site:	Soccer field or large open field suitable for soccer, set up for a regular soccer game with boundaries and goals, etc.
Object of the Game:	To have your team make the most goals.

To Play:

The players are divided into two teams. Players on each team pair up and tie their legs together in "three-legged race" fashion, i.e., two players stand side-by-side and tie their adjacent legs together so that they must move their inside legs in unison.

Goalies may be tied together back-to-back at the waist.

Regular soccer rules and procedure are followed.

Variation:

Use two or more balls.

Comments:

If there is an odd number of players, one person can be a referee-scorekeeper. Other players can take turns filling this role.

Purpose or Benefit

This is a creative variation to traditional soccer which exercises players' coordination and cooperation.

Annihilation

Number of Players:	10-20
Length of Time:	20-90 minutes
Materials:	2 large buckets or baskets A ball which fits into the buckets, yet is not smaller than a volleyball
Playing Site:	Large open area
Preparation:	Establish boundaries which are approximately 20 yards long and 15 yards wide. The buckets are buried to the rims at each end of the field.
Object of the Game:	To score more goals than the opponents.

To Play:

Players are divided into two equal teams. A goalie is appointed for each. He should remain close to his team's goal in order to defend it when necessary.

The ball is placed in the middle of the playing area. Both teams line up on their knees at the ends of the field beside the goals which they are respectively defending. At the signal, both teams pursue the ball while remaining throughout the entire game on their knees.

The teams attempt by any means possible to move the ball so as to ultimately score by putting the ball in the proper bucket. To facilitate scoring, the goalie may be physically removed from the area around the goal.

To gain possession of the ball from an opponent, there are virtually no restrictions on what players are allowed to do.

If any part of a player's body goes out-of-bounds, he is taken out of the game.

If the ball goes out-of-bounds, the team that did *not* touch it last gains possession.

All action is called to a halt when a massive "jam-up" occurs which lasts for more than one minute. Play is resumed by having the teams line up and, at the signal, pursuing the ball as at the start of the game.

Comments:

Knee pads or heavy-duty pants are recommended to preserve players' knees.

Purpose or Benefit

"Annihilation" builds strength, endurance, and provides a unique and refreshingly unrestrained, yet disciplined, competition.

Bad Pass

Number of Players:	4-25
Length of Time:	15-45 minutes
Materials:	Small toy ball A chair for each player (optional)
Playing Site:	Large open area
Object of the Game:	To be the last player not disqualified by either a bad throw or a bad catch.

To Play:

Players are seated in chairs or on the floor in a circle. All players face the center, with one person holding the ball.

The player with the ball tries to throw the trickiest pass he can at any of the other players. If the pass is catchable, i.e., thrown in such a way that it could be reasonably caught, and the receiver misses it, then the receiver is out of the game and leaves the circle.

A player is likewise eliminated if he throws an uncatchable pass. The validity of a pass is determined by the group's consensus or a designated referee.

After each elimination, play resumes until one player remains, who is the winner.

Variation:

Use more than one ball simultaneously.

Comments:

Besides including tricky passes (e.g., looking one way and throwing another), the passes should be thrown in rapid succession. The ball should be kept moving quickly, but should not be thrown fast or hard.

Purpose or Benefit

"Bad Pass" is fast-paced, requires attentiveness, and provides practice in passing and receiving.

Fool Ball

Number of Players:	8-20
Length of Time:	15-45 minutes
Material:	A ball
Playing Site:	Large open area
Object of the Game:	To catch the ball and not move to catch it unless the ball has been thrown.

To Play:

One player, holding the ball, stands in the center of a circle that the other players have formed; they are also standing.

The players in the circle have their hands behind their backs. The person with the ball indicates to whom he will throw the ball first, and which direction around the circle he will continue in, throwing the ball to each player by turn.

The player to whom the ball is to be thrown must reach for the ball only if the ball is actually thrown. If he moves his hands to catch the ball when it is not thrown, or if he fails to catch the ball when it is thrown, he is out of the game. A player who is out of the game sits down or stands with his arms folded across his chest. If the ball is thrown poorly, a player is not eliminated for not catching it.

The player in the middle may throw the ball to the next player immediately, or he may bluff, pretending to throw the ball, trying to fool the player.

When all but one of the players in the circle are out of the game, the last player remaining becomes the person in the middle with the ball.

Purpose or Benefit

"Fool Ball" challenges players to practice self-control and attentiveness.

Four Square

Number of Players:	5-12
Length of Time:	20-60 minutes
Materials:	Four-square ball or volleyball Masking tape or chalk
Playing Site:	Flat, hard surface, indoors or outdoors, with a minimum of 16' x 16', so players have room to maneuver. A clean surface is best.
Preparation:	Mark 7' to 8' section of floor with masking tape or chalk, forming a square subdivided into 4 equal-sized squares of $3^{1}/_{2}$' to 4'. Crayon or paint may be used to more permanently mark a four-square court on a concrete surface.
Object of the Game:	To gain the #1 square and defend the position against the other three attackers.

To Play:

One of the four squares is designated as the #1 square. The remaining three squares are sequentially numbered in a clockwise direction. Then four players begin the game, while the rest wait in line. Each of the four players guards his own square.

The player of the #1 square always serves the ball. He bounces the ball inside his square, then hits it with an open palm of either hand into one of the other squares. The ball typically bounces one time in the new square and then the person who guards that square must direct it to another square of his choice. Soft taps are allowed. Each time, the ball must bounce no more than once in a given square (the ball can be deflected in midair without a bounce).

This continues until someone fails to return the ball to another person's square. At that point he leaves the playing area and goes to the end of the waiting line, and the person at the front of the waiting line goes to the #4 square. The players shift around, if necessary, so that each person guards a single square. For example, if the #2 person goes out, the #3 person now guards the #2 square, and the old #4 player now guards the #3 square. The newest person always guards the #4 square.

A common strategy is to try to eliminate the players in squares in front of one so that one can move closer to the #1 square. Players normally straddle the corners of their squares and lean in, because if they are hit with the ball while standing in their squares they are out.

Other rules are as follows:

1. Hitting with a closed hand is not allowed, as the ball will travel at an unfair rate of speed.

2. If the ball bounces on the outside line, the player who hit it there leaves the playing area.

3. If the ball bounces between 2 squares, the other players and those waiting in line can help decide whose square it was in.

4. If a person catches the ball, he is out.

5. If a ball doesn't bounce in the square served to, and the defender doesn't return it, the last person to touch the ball is out.

Purpose or Benefit

"Four Square" improves coordination, agility, and reaction time.

Fox and Squirrel

Number of Players: 8-20

Length of Time: 15-45 minutes

Materials: 3 balls: 2 similar balls and one smaller, distinctly different ball

Playing Site: Large open area

Object of the Game: The foxes try to catch the squirrel by tagging whoever is holding the squirrel ball with one or both of the fox balls.

To Play:

Players stand in a circle and pass the fox balls (the two larger balls) from player to player. The fox balls must be passed to the next player but can go in either direction, or be reversed. The squirrel ball (the smaller ball) can be thrown to anyone in the circle.

The players call out "Fox" or "Squirrel" as they pass one of the balls. When a player has a "fox" ball, he can throw it at a player holding a "squirrel" ball to tag him. The game may be played as an elimination game with "squirrels" going out when they are tagged by "foxes." The game is fun with or without elimination.

Purpose or Benefit

"Fox and Squirrel" is exciting and requires quick thinking and reacting.

Hot Potato

Number of Players: 5-20

Length of Time: 15-30 minutes

Material: A ball the size of a volleyball

Object of the Game: To not get caught with the ball.

To Play:

The players stand or sit in a circle, with one player in the center. One player in the circle holds the ball.

The ball is passed around the circle. The player in the center can at any time call out "hot potato." The player with the ball at that moment goes into the center in place of the other player, and the game continues until everyone has been in the center.

Comments:

This is a good children's game.

Purpose or Benefit

This game takes coordination, helps develop good reflexes, and keeps the players in suspense.

Poof Ball

Number of Players: 4-20

Length of Time: 15-60 minutes

Materials: Large, long table
                        Ping-pong ball
                        Masking tape

Object of the Game: To blow the ball off the table on the opponent's side.

To Play:

Players are divided into two teams at opposite sides of the

table. A line midway between them is indicated with masking tape. Players decide upon the winning score before the game starts (10-15 points is reasonable).

The ball is placed in the center of the table. At a signal, the players begin to blow the ball. Players may not touch the table with their hands, nor the ball with their lips. Heads must not extend over the surface of the table. A point is given the team that blows the ball off the opposite team's side. After one to five points have been scored (it can vary) the teams rotate their players. The first team to reach the predetermined score wins.

Variations:

1. In large groups, it is possible to divide into teams of five and have a tournament.

2. In small groups, barriers can be set up at the ends of the table, thus limiting the area through which goals can be scored and also limiting the area that needs to be guarded. If the ball goes over the barrier, a point is scored for the opposing team.

Comments:

Players will appreciate an opportunity to catch their breath between games! Use a smaller table for children since they cannot blow as hard.

Purpose or Benefit

This game is an exciting crowd-pleaser. It is goal-oriented and requires lots of breath control.

Slaughter

Number of Players:	8-30
Length of Time:	20-60 minutes
Materials:	2 rubber playground balls (volleyballs are acceptable) 1 roll of masking tape

Playing Site: Gymnasium or other large room

Preparation: A strip of masking tape is laid across
                     the center of the room, the full width
                     of the floor.

Object of the Game: To take the opponents out of the
                     game by hitting them with the ball.

To Play:

The players are divided into two equal teams. Each team is
assigned to one side of the court. The area behind the tape is
off-limits to everyone except the team which has been assigned to that end of the court. If a player enters the area
which is off-limits to him, he must leave the game.

A ball is given to each team and, on signal, the players are free
to roam around and throw the balls at their opponents. If a
person is hit with the ball, he leaves the game, unless he or a
teammate catches the ball before it hits the floor.

Anytime a ball is caught before it hits either the floor or the
wall, the person who threw it leaves the game.

It is permissible to deflect a thrown ball with a ball that is being held.

The game ends when an entire team has been removed from
the game.

Variations:

1. "Slaughter" can be played without off-limits areas.

2. Any number of balls can be used.

3. Players who were removed from the game may be brought
   back in when a teammate catches a ball before it hits either
   the floor or the wall.

Purpose or Benefit

"Slaughter" involves throwing and catching skills, and generally being alert.

MODERATELY PHYSICALLY ACTIVE GAMES

Here are a variety of games requiring a moderate amount of physical activity. Most are *indoor games*. Some can be adapted to outdoor play. A few are good *outdoor games*, such as "Trust Walk," "Group Lap," and "Hagoo." This section includes:

> Variations of Musical Chairs
> "Trust" Games
> Laughter Games

Variations of Musical Chairs

Face-to-Face

Number of Players:	6-20
Length of Time:	10-30 minutes
Materials:	If a record player or piano are available, the game can be played with music, but this is not required.
Playing Site:	A room with enough space for players to be a good distance apart from one another and move easily about the room.
Object of the Game:	To quickly find a partner before they are all taken when the signal is given.

To Play:

Each player is assigned a partner by the leader. The leader may play music (optional) and begin calling out instructions as to how the partners must face each other.

For example, if he calls out "face to face," they stand opposite each other, looking at each other. He can call out things such as "side to side," "back to back," "elbow to elbow," "thumb to thumb," "right hand to left hand," etc.

At some point he stops the music, or calls out (if no music is used), "Everyone change partners!" At this point each person, including the leader, must find a new partner. The person left without a partner is the new leader who calls out the directions.

As the game goes on, it can be more challenging if the rule is that each person must find a partner he has not had before.

Comments:

If the group is mixed with younger and older children, it may be helpful to pair up, at least at first, older with younger children so that the younger ones receive help in knowing what positions to take as the directions are called out. For groups of older children, boys and girls may be resistant to playing with each other.

"Face-to-Face" is a lively game which helps people to intermingle. For children, it can be an exercise in following and giving instructions. For younger children, it is good practice in identifying parts of the body.

Fruit Basket

Number of Players: 7-20

Length of Time: 10-30 minutes

Playing Site: Arrange chairs in a circle for all but one player

Object of the Game: To keep from being "it."

To Play:

Players are seated in a circle. A person designated as "it" stands in the center.

The names of several fruits are selected, one fruit for every three to four players. Each is assigned a fruit. The player who is "it" calls out the name of a fruit. All players with that fruit must find a new seat (from the ones the others with that fruit have been in) before the player who is "it" finds a chair. The one who is left without a chair is the new "it." "It" may also call, "Fruit basket," in which case *all* players must move to a new chair.

Variations:

Other categories may be used instead of fruit, e.g., Scripture characters, fruit of the Spirit, months, etc.

"Fruit Basket" is active and spirited. It frees people from inhibitions and is a good ice-breaker.

Jungle Safari Hunt

Number of Players: 4-20

Length of Time: 15-30 minutes

Playing Site: Arrange chairs in a circle, with one less chair than the number of players and ample space in the circle's center for each player to move around.

Preparation: The leader of the game prepares a list of animals, birds or other jungle creatures, one for each player. He may prepare in advance a story about a "jungle safari hunt" which uses the name of each animal, or make it up at the time.

Object of the Game: To find a chair when the hunter comes before they are all gone.

To Play:

Each player takes the name of an animal and its appropriate action or sound (e.g., a lion roaring, snake hissing, alligator snapping, owl hooting, etc.). These can be assigned by the leader or written on slips of paper and drawn by everyone. The animals wait their turn outside the circle of chairs.

The leader proceeds to tell his story. When an animal is mentioned, the player with that identity comes to the center of the circle and does his action.

For example, the leader says, "We went on a jungle safari in Africa. When we entered the jungle, the first thing we heard was a snake hissing." At this point, the snake slinks or crawls to the center of the circle making hissing sounds.

After the player enters the circle and performs his action or sound, he takes a chair. The game proceeds in this way until the last animal is in the center of the circle. The leader then says in the story, "The HUNTER is coming!" At this point all players must find a new chair. The player left without a chair becomes the new leader.

The game is repeated and everyone draws a new animal's name. Or, entirely different animals may be selected by the new leader who must come up with a story using them.

Children especially enjoy acting out the animal's parts and the excitement of "Jungle Safari Hunt."

Mailman

Number of Players:	5-12
Length of Time:	10-30 minutes
Materials:	Some envelopes, leaflets or papers to serve as the "mail" Chair for each player One Blindfold
Playing Site:	Fairly large room with a chair for each player except the "mailman." Arrange the chairs in different spots around the room.
Object of the Game:	For the mailman: to intercept the mail. For the players: to pass the mail on to the next destination without being intercepted by the mailman.

To Play:

A piece of mail is distributed to each player except the mailman. One person is the "mailman" and is blindfolded. Each player takes the name of a place and sits in a chair. One of the players is the "conductor" and calls out, "THE MAIL IS GOING FROM _____ to _____," choosing two of the players' places.

The two players called must change places and exchange the mail in the process without being intercepted by the mailman. If the mailman succeeds in intercepting a piece of the mail, he changes places with the person who had it, and that person becomes the mailman.

Variation:

To make the game more difficult for older children, players are blindfolded and the two "places" must find each other without being able to see.

Comments:

A game especially suitable for children 5-12 years of age.

Purpose or Benefit

"Mailman" is active but not rowdy. Because children are each in their own chairs they are easily controlled.

Musical Balloons

Number of Players:	6-25
Length of Time:	30 minutes
Materials:	Balloons, enough for all but one player A record player
Object of the Game:	To have a balloon in your hands when the music stops.

To Play:

The players stand in a circle, all but one holding a balloon. Another person is in charge of the record player.

The record player is started and all the players start passing balloons, all in the same direction. When the music stops (the person at the record player lifts the needle), the player who does not have a balloon in his hands is out of the game.

Also, if a balloon pops, the person holding it is out of the game. A balloon is taken out each time a player goes out. The game continues until the winner is left.

Purpose or Benefit

Coordination and quick reflexes are required for "Musical Balloons." It is also suspenseful.

Musical Hats

Number of Players: 6-25

Length of Time: 15-30 minutes

Materials: One hat for all but one player.
Any source of music that can be stopped abruptly—record player, radio, piano, etc.

Object of the Game: To have a hat on your head when the music stops.

To Play:

All the players stand or sit in a circle. All of them except one put hats on their heads. Another person controls the music.

Each player passes the hat on his head to the person next to him and places the hat passed to him on his own head (passing must be all in the same direction). The players continue to pass the hats this way, fairly quickly, not having more than one hat in their possession at a time.

The player without a hat when the music stops is eliminated from the game, along with one of the hats. The game continues until there is only one player left, who is the winner.

Variations:

1. Each player removes the hat of the person sitting next to him instead of waiting for him to pass it.

2. Each player passes his hat by placing it on the head of the person next to him.

Comments:

"Musical Hats" is most amusing when played with a variety of styles of hats.

Purpose or Benefit

"Musical Hats" is humorous, suspenseful, and a good exercise in coordination.

Trust Circle

Number of Players: 9-15 (3-15 for "Courage Camille" variation)

Length of Time: 15-30 minutes

Playing Site: Area large enough for players to stand in a circle, arms linked

Object of the Game: To hold up the person in the middle and keep him safe from falling.

To Play:

One player is chosen to be "it" first. A tight circle of players is formed, alternating physically strong and weak people. The person chosen to be "it" goes into the middle of the circle and crosses his arms across his chest.

The "it" stiffens and falls backwards. The players in the circle work together to catch the person and pass him back and forth around the circle. The player in the middle must keep his feet together and near the middle of the circle for this to work well, and players in the circle generally grab the person who is "it" around the arms and shoulders. Each player is encouraged to have a turn.

Variations:

1. Players in the circle sit down, placing their feet around the ankles of the person in the middle. This makes the game a bit more exciting and challenging.

2. "Courage Camille" is a slight variation of this game in which only 3 players are required. Two of the players face each other and lock hands. The third person stiffens and falls backwards into their arms. This should be done several times, with the person falling farther backwards each time (the players locking their hands should lower them each time). Other players can then try.

3. "Courage Camille" can also be played with only one person catching.

4. The person who is "it" wears a blindfold.

Comments:

The players who are "catchers" should exercise care as they pass the person around and catch him. In the "Courage Camille" variation, care should be taken that the two players who are acting as "catchers" are strong enough to hold the heaviest person participating.

Purpose or Benefit

"Trust Circle" provides a unique opportunity for players to learn to trust each other in a concrete way. It also fosters unity among the participants in the circle.

Trust Lift

Number of Players:	9-15
Length of Time:	5-30 minutes
Playing Site:	Area large enough for players to stand in a circle. If playing inside, the ceiling should be at least 9 feet above the floor
Object of the Game:	To lift a person above everyone's head.

To Play:

One player is chosen to be "it" first. He lies on his back and stiffens himself while everyone else assembles around him. Together everyone lifts him slowly toward the ceiling as he maintains his reclining position. Once he has reached maximum height, the others hold him there for about 30 seconds before slowly lowering him.

Purpose or Benefit

"Trust Lift" provides a good opportunity for participants to develop trust in each other.

Trust Walk

Number of Players:	2-20
Length of Time:	20-60 minutes
Material:	Blindfolds
Physical Set-up:	A large area in which to walk—outdoors or a large house in which you can use all the rooms
Object of the Game:	For the person who is blindfolded to grow in trust of the person who is leading, and for the "leader" to grow in sensitivity and concern for the blindfolded person.

To Play:

The group is divided into pairs. One person in each pair becomes the "leader." An amount of time is specified for how long the walk should take.

The leader takes the "follower's" hand and they go for a walk. Halfway through the allotted time they switch roles and the leader is then blindfolded and becomes the follower.

When everyone returns to the large group, a time for reporting experiences and impressions is often fun and fruitful.

Variations:

1. The leader may wish to place various objects in the follower's hands and see if he can discover what these things are through senses other than sight (touch, smell, etc.). The leader should look for things which would stimulate and heighten the follower's awareness of his other four senses. This variation then becomes a "Discovery Walk" as well as a "Trust Walk."

2. Obstacles can be set up around which the leader will guide the follower.

Comments:

If there is not an even number of players, one group can be a threesome with one person guiding two followers.

Because the object of the game is to build trust between persons, an exhortation may be needed at the beginning to not play practical jokes on the blindfolded persons!

Purpose or Benefit

The experience of "Trust Walk" builds trust in others, helps participants appreciate God's creation by experiencing it through other senses, heightens awareness of surroundings, and builds unity through the sharing of a common experience. It also provides an opportunity for pairs of people to get to know one another and deepen their relationships.

Laughter Games

Drop the Handkerchief

Number of Players: 4-50

Length of Time: 2-10 minutes

Materials: Handkerchief

Object of the Game: As a group, to stop laughing when the handkerchief hits the ground. There are no winners or losers.

To Play:

As the leader tosses the handkerchief into the air, the whole group starts laughing. They are to stop laughing at the instant the handkerchief touches the ground.

The toss can be repeated several times, varying the manner in which it is thrown.

Purpose or Benefit

"Drop the Handkerchief" is good for occupying and stimulating a group of children for a few minutes, and also presents a challenge to adults. It is a good exercise for releasing inhibitions.

Group Lap

Number of Players:	15-50
Length of Time:	10-30 minutes
Playing Site:	Large open area
Object of the Game:	To form a circle of people, each sitting on the lap of the person behind him.

To Play:

Players form a large circle, then turn so they are in single file. They should be fairly close together.

On a signal they all slowly bend to a sitting position where each can balance, sitting on the lap of the person behind, while the person in front sits on his lap. This requires coordination and proper spacing, and may take several attempts.

Once this is achieved, and players have their balance, they may attempt to walk. One player tells the group which foot to start with and counts to three. Players simultaneously move one foot slowly, then the other.

Comments:

This game is especially good for children and teenagers, preferably of the same sex. Those who are able to walk in this position have really accomplished something.

Purpose or Benefit

"Group Lap" builds a sense of unity and togetherness in a group.

Hagoo

Number of Players:	10-30
Length of Time:	20-60 minutes
Object of the Game:	To walk the gauntlet without smiling or laughing.

To Play:

Players are divided into two teams which line up in rows facing each other, forming the gauntlet. Two players, one from each team, stand at opposite ends of the gauntlet and bow to each other, calling "Hagoo." "Hagoo" means "come here" in the language of the Flingit Indians of Alaska, who invented the game.

The two players walk toward each other maintaining eye contact, then pass each other and walk to the end of the line. Both players try to keep a straight face the whole time.

In the meantime, players forming the gauntlet are trying their best to make the challengers laugh. Touching the challengers is forbidden.

The challengers who run the gauntlet successfully rejoin their own team. Those who smile or laugh join the opposing team.

The game ends when there is only one team, or when the players can take no more.

Purpose or Benefit

This game allows everyone to try his best jokes and funny faces in an appropriate setting. It is also an excellent exercise in self-control.

Noah's Ark

Number of Players:	20-100
Length of Time:	15-30 minutes
Materials:	Slips of paper with animal names on them, 2 slips for each animal
Preparation:	Animal names are written on slips of paper, two slips for each animal, and enough for each person in the group to have one. The slips are distributed.
Object of the Game:	To find the other person with the name of your animal.

To Play:

All walk around, making the noises of their respective animals, until each finds the other person who was given the same animal.

Variations:

1. More than two slips are made for each animal, in order to divide the participants into groups.

2. Pictures of animals are used, especially for children who cannot read.

3. Players do not make their animal's noises, but question each other to see who has their matching animal.

Purpose or Benefit

"Noah's Ark" is great for helping people in a large group to get to know each other. It can also serve as a way to pair people for a succeeding game which requires partners.

Poor Kitty

Number of Players:	5-12
Length of Time:	15-45 minutes
Object of the Game:	To keep a straight face.

To Play:

One player is chosen as the "kitty" and goes to the center of the circle. The kitty begins to act like a cat and approaches one of the seated players, who must stroke the kitty's head and say "poor kitty" three times without smiling or laughing. The kitty is free to make faces at the person stroking.

According to the players' preference, either the first person or the last person to laugh becomes the next kitty.

Variation:

Other animals are imitated, such as "poor piggy," "poor elephant," or "poor puppy," etc. Animals that make noise and have peculiar behaviors are best.

Comments:

Players should be encouraged to really "ham it up" to help induce laughter.

Purpose or Benefit

"Poor Kitty" challenges self-control. It can also relax the players' inhibitions.

CREATIVE-DRAMATIC GAMES

Creative-Dramatic games include:

> Artistic Games
> Dramatic Games
> Musical Games
> Storytelling Games

Although all the games involve some kind of art, drama, music or storytelling, most *do not require any special skill* in these areas! The dramatic, musical and storytelling games can draw upon players' experience in these areas but will also be enjoyed by players of little or no expertise.

"Create a Song" and "Orchestra" take more skill than the other games. However, if "unskilled" players are teamed with those who have some skills, they often enjoy these games.

Create a Creature

Number of Players:	3-12
Length of Time:	10-30 minutes
Materials:	Fairly large sheets of paper Pencils/crayons
Playing Site:	Players sit in separate chairs around the room
Object of the game:	To create a "creature" together that is amusing.

To Play:

The first player draws the head of a person, animal, bird, etc., at the top of a piece of paper. He folds the paper over so that what he has drawn cannot be seen by the next player. He makes a mark, however, indicating where the neck attaches.

The next player draws a body, folds the paper so that what he has drawn cannot be seen by the next "artist," and marks where the legs attach.

The last player draws legs and/or feet, tail, etc. (whatever finishing touches he wants to add).

Comments:

As no one knows what the persons before them have drawn, the resulting creature they create together causes laughter and entertainment.

Purpose or Benefit

A noncompetitive, entertaining game that involves creativity. This game gives people an opportunity to draw in a nonthreatening situation, no special artistic skills are required and the result is amusing.

Dough Art

Number of Players:	1-10
Length of Time:	1-2 hours
Materials:	Dough ingredients (recipe in "Preparation")
	Paints for decorating
	Varnish
	Rolling pin
	Foil-covered cookie sheet
	Surface to roll out dough
	Oven
Preparation:	Prepare dough ahead of time: mix 2 cups of flour, 1 cup of salt, and 1 cup of water. Knead 7-10 minutes until smooth. The dough can be kept in plastic bags to prevent drying, but is best used immediately.
Object of the Game:	To create something from the dough (beads, ornaments, baskets, plaques, etc.).

To Play:

The dough is rolled out to $1/4$", then shapes are cut out with cookie cutters or original shapes are created. Thin objects usually turn out better than thick. If pieces of dough are moistened, they will stick together.

The shapes are placed on a foil-covered cookie sheet and baked $1/2$ hour for every $1/4$" of dough thickness (or until golden brown) at 325°-350°.

To finish, several types of paints may be used (water colors, poster, etc.). A sealer of some sort must always be applied (e.g., varnish or enamel paint), otherwise sculptures could be affected by moisture or humidity.

Comments:

A leader could direct a group with a specific purpose or occasion in mind.

Children can successfully do dough art, though younger children need more guidance.

"Dough Art" is quiet and creative. It gives a sense of accomplishment when completed.

It can also be used for practical purposes such as making gifts, centerpieces, ornaments, jewelry, etc.

Draw a Duck

Number of Players:	3-30
Length of Time:	15-60 minutes
Materials:	Paper (one sheet per player) Pen or pencil Blindfold
Object of the Game:	To draw a duck or a good semblance thereof.

To Play:

Each person, in turn, is blindfolded, spun around three times, given paper and pencil and instructed to draw a duck. The duck's eye and tail must be included in the drawing.

The results are usually hilarious.

Variation:

Especially with larger groups, after several people have drawn, the animal is changed (to a dog, for example) to minimize players' learning from each other's drawings.

Purpose or Benefit

"Draw a Duck" is light, simple, and humorous. It is good for encouraging new people to participate.

Draw in the Dark

Number of Players:	2-20
Length of Time:	15-30 minutes
Materials:	Paper (a sheet for each player)
	Pens or pencils
	Hard surface for drawing
Preparation:	Each person is supplied with paper, pencil, and a writing surface.
Object of the Game:	To draw a picture.

To Play:

The lights are turned off. Each person draws a picture within a certain time limit. The lights are turned on so all can see what they've done.

Variation:

Participants may be required to draw a specified subject.

Purpose or Benefit

"Draw in the Dark" is a challenging, creative, and humorous activity.

Group Construction

Number of Players:	6-18
Length of Time:	25 minutes
Materials:	Wooden toy blocks
	Tinkertoys
	Blindfold for each person
	Prepared diagrams of Christian symbols
Preparation:	Diagrams are prepared, usually pictures containing several Christian symbols arranged to look like emblems. Examples are on the next page:

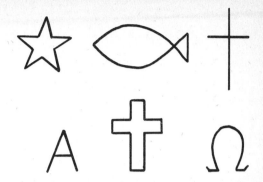

| Object of the Game: | To reconstruct the diagram with blocks and tinkertoys, without looking. |

To Play:

Players are divided into groups of two to four persons. Each group is given a diagram to study. With blindfolds on, each group tries to reconstruct its diagram with tinkertoys and blocks.

After 15 minutes players compare their results with the original designs.

Purpose or Benefit

Participants grow in learning teamwork by "Group Construction." Memory, design and construction abilities are fostered.

Scribbles

Number of Players:	2-20
Length of Time:	30-60 minutes
Materials:	Pencils
	Pens
	Paper
	Coloring media (i.e. crayons, colored pencils, felt pens, etc.)

122

Preparation: The leader draws a simple scribble on
                          a piece of paper for each participant.

Object of the Game: To draw pictures from a scribble.

To Play:

A scribble is given to each person. Drawing utensils are made available.

Players are instructed to draw and color a picture incorporating the scribble in some way into their drawing.

Players can be instructed to draw:
1. Any kind of tree or flower.
2. A picture of themselves as reflected from the back of a spoon.
3. "Your own thing," i.e., anything you want to draw.
4. A "doodle."
5. A person or animal of any kind.

Players all show their pictures to each other when they are finished. An "art gallery" can be created by posting these "priceless" originals. Products may be humorous.

Comments:

Time limits may be set for each picture drawn.

After the first pictures are drawn, another person can be the leader, drawing a scribble for each person and giving his own instructions.

Purpose or Benefit

"Scribbles" provides an opportunity to be creative, and interact with each other. This is an artistic activity that can be participated in without having artistic talent.

Scripture Artist

Number of Players: 6-24
Length of Time: 30-60 minutes

Materials:	Pencils
	Pad of scratch paper for each team
Preparation:	Familiar Bible verses are written out on small pieces of paper, folded, and put into a bowl or bag.
Object of the Game:	To guess what Scripture verse a picture portrays.

To Play:

Players are separated into teams of 3-4 people.

The teams are situated in different areas of the room (out of earshot of each other is best).

One person from each team goes to the bowl. He takes a paper and reads it silently. He returns to his own team and begins drawing (no letters or numbers) to illustrate the saying. The artist may not speak.

The rest of each team tries to guess the verse. The first team to guess wins. Then another person from each team goes to select a verse. The process continues until all have drawn. The team to finish first wins.

Variation:

"Book Covers": Instead of Bible verses, book titles are portrayed.

Comments:

Use Scripture verses or book titles that are somewhat familiar to all.

Purpose or Benefit

"Scripture Artist" is exciting and challenges creativity.

Dramatic Games

Charades

Number of Players: 4-20

Length of Time: 20 minutes-2 hours

Materials: Paper and pencils
Clock or watch with second hand

Object of the Game: To communicate a word or phrase nonverbally.

To Play:

Players are divided into two teams of equal size and are sent to separate rooms to deliberate. Each team must decide on titles of songs, movies or books that the other team will be given to dramatize. A title is written on a small piece of paper for each member of the other team. The papers are folded and collected.

When the teams reunite, someone begins by picking one of the papers that the opposite team has prepared. After reading it silently, he tries to communicate the word or phrase to his teammates without speaking. A member of the opposite team keeps track of the time.

Before the action begins, however, all players should understand the signals available. Usually the actor begins by demonstrating the category of his title: If it is a movie, he pretends to be taking a movie; if a book, he puts his hands in front of him, palms up and side by side; if a song, he puts his hand to his mouth and then extends his arm.

He indicates the number of words in the title by holding up the same number of fingers, then indicates which word he will begin acting out by holding up the number of fingers corresponding to the word's position in the phrase, e.g., three fingers means the third word. If he is going to act out the whole title, he draws a circle in the air or forms a circle with his thumb and forefinger. The actor may indicate the number of syllables in a particular word by extending the appropriate number of fingers and patting them on his opposite arm. He then repeats the gesture to indicate which syllable of the word he will demonstrate.

Other gestures may aid communication. The actor holds out his thumb and index finger, slightly separated, to mean "little word," such as "in," "the," "to," etc. He may pull at his earlobe to mean "sounds like," which means the word he is going to act out rhymes with a word in the title or sounds similar in some other way.

The actor may use any combination of these signals along with his own pantomiming, as long as he does not use his voice. His teammates, however, may speak freely, trying to understand and put the right words together. When one of them hits on the right word or words the actor nods and/or points to the person who guessed correctly. If someone says a word that is nearly right, the actor makes a beckoning gesture so that the player will know he is on the right track. If the guessing is completely wrong, he waves them off.

The actor is free to go on to a new word or a new approach at any time, whether or not his teammates guessed the last one he tried to communicate. Likewise, his teammates may try to guess the whole title at any time and suffer no penalty for an incorrect guess.

When a player correctly guesses the title, the timekeeper records the time. If three minutes pass before the team has guessed correctly, the timekeeper calls time, and the time is recorded as three minutes. The actor may then reveal his subject.

The group may also decide on warning points for the timekeeper to announce, such as 60 and 30 seconds before the three minutes are expired.

The teams alternate sending a member to draw one of the other team's papers until everyone has been the actor once. The team with lowest total time wins.

Variations:

1. Other categories are acceptable subjects, such as Bible characters, occupations, famous sayings, daily activities, etc.

2. Charades are performed on group, rather than team basis, with the subjects to be acted out being prepared before-

hand, or decided on spontaneously by the actors.

3. Especially in small groups, the teams may prepare two or three subjects for each person on the other team to enact.

4. "Paper Charades": Duplicate titles (or phrases, subjects, etc.) are given to one player on each team at the same time. These players then proceed to *illustrate* clues for their teams. The team which guesses first is the winner of that round. For example, a player might draw a picture of an open book and a whale in order to get his particular team to guess *Moby Dick*.

5. "Proverbs Charades": Quotations from the book of Proverbs are used. A word limit should be determined prior to the game in order to avoid unduly long quotes (suggested maximum 10-15 words). Each team is given a 5-minute limit in which to guess the charade.

Comments:

When subjects for the charades are being selected, care should be taken to use titles, etc., that are well-known, but still challenging to communicate.

Also, several teams can play the variation "Paper Charades" at once, if many people are present; everyone would get a chance to draw in a shorter amount of time than in regular charades.

Purpose or Benefit

Players are challenged to creativity as they receive encouragement from their teammates and relax their social inhibitions. Players use their imaginations in problem-solving.

Do It This Way

Number of Players:	5-15
Length of Time:	20-60 minutes
Object of the Game:	To guess the secret adverb that the group has chosen.

To Play:

One player leaves the room. The others decide on the secret adverb (e.g., slowly, carefully, quickly, energetically, etc.). The absent player returns and tells each person, "Do it this way."

For example, he may tell the first person, "Eat this way." The person then pantomimes eating in the manner of the adverb (e.g., eat slowly, carefully, etc.). He can tell each person to do a different thing "this way," such as walk, comb your hair, read a book, etc.

The person receives 10 guesses. If he guesses the adverb after the first person "does it this way," he gets 10 points, and one less point for each person after that.

Variations:

1. The game can be played by teams. Each team selects a secret adverb for the other team to guess. To do this, the teams go to separate rooms and form a list, then take turns asking each other to "do it this way" as they go down their lists. The scoring system is the same, only the entire team is allowed to guess instead of just individuals.

2. "Guess the Invisible Object": Instead of a secret adverb, an object is chosen. The team then pantomimes passing the object to one another in a way that will indicate what it is.

Purpose or Benefit

"Do It This Way" provides an opportunity to be creative and dramatic through a simple exercise in pantomime.

Expressing the Psalms

Number of Players:	5-15
Length of Time:	45-90 minutes
Materials:	Bible for each player
Object of the Game:	To personally express what a psalm means in a creative way.

To Play:

Each player selects a psalm to portray in any way he chooses
(e.g., dramatize, draw, sing, read with added narration, etc.).

After preparation, players gather together and express/per-
form their chosen psalm for each other.

Variation:

Players express the psalms in pairs or small groups instead of
individually.

Purpose or Benefit

This activity calls upon creative abilities and is very edifying.

Machine Charades

Number of Players: 6-30

Length of Time: 20-60 minutes

Object of the Game: To guess what machine a team is acting out.

To Play:

The group is divided into equal teams.

Each team goes to separate rooms and decides as a group what
machine they will act out, and how they will do it. They may
decide and rehearse more than one machine, depending on
how long the game is to be played.

Each person on the team makes up a part of the machine. One
person may be the operator of the machine.

The teams come back together and each presents their "machine" to the other teams. The audience guesses what the
other team's machine is after they have finished acting it out.

Variation:

Instead of dividing into teams, one person simply begins being
part of a machine. When somone thinks he knows what the

machine is, he acts out another part. They continue until all are functioning parts of the machine. It may be discovered afterwards that everyone was not thinking of the same machine.

Purpose or Benefit

"Machine Charades" is a challenging, creative, lose-your-inhibitions game.

Mimic the Leader

Number of Players: 5-25

Length of Time: 15 minutes

Object of the Game: To guess what the leader is doing.

To Play:

One person is designated the actor and is sent out of the room. While he is gone, the leader acts something out, e.g., flying a kite. He tells everyone in the room what he is doing.

The actor is called back into the room. The leader does his act and the actor mimics him and must guess what he has just done.

Everyone takes a turn at being the actor and the leader.

Purpose or Benefit

"Mimic the Leader" challenges the imagination and is a simple exercise in pantomime. It is a good game for children and adults.

Paper-Bag Skits

Number of Players: 6-30

Length of Time: 60-90 minutes

Materials:	Large paper bags
	Assorted household objects

Preparation: A paper bag for each group is filled in advance with five unrelated objects.

Object of the Game: To create a skit using specific objects.

To Play:

Players are divided into groups of three to six. A filled paper bag is given to each group. The groups then go to separate places and each prepares/creates a skit using the five objects.

The objects may or may not be used for their normal functions. Each object must be used and each player must participate.

After the skit is planned and rehearsed (20-30 minutes), the groups return and perform for one another.

Variations:

1. Stipulations are given regarding the type of skits performed, e.g., humorous, serious, acting out a parable, a moral, or a proverb.

2. Five bags are prepared, one labelled "who," another labelled "what," another "when," another "where," another "why." In each bag are placed pieces of paper with information appropriate to the bag's category, e.g., "where" would have a different location written on each piece of paper. Each individual or group draws a paper from each of the five bags. They then act out a short scene or story using the five given components—with or without rehearsal. Lots of encouragement should be given to the actors.

Purpose or Benefit

It is entertaining for all, uses creative abilities, and is a good way to be able to interact with new people.

Personified Toy Box

Number of Players:	5-15
Length of Time:	20-60 minutes
Preparation:	Names of toys are written in advance on slips of paper, one for each player.
Object of the Game:	To guess what toy is being described.

To Play:

The papers indicating toys are distributed. Players look at them and think of clues to help the other players guess what they are.

A player starts the game by making a statement about himself as if he were the toy, and as if the toy were a person, e.g., "I have a bouncy personality."

The other players attempt to guess what toy he is. The first player to guess correctly gets a point. However, if a person makes an incorrect guess, he eliminates himself from that round.

If no one guesses correctly, the toy gives another clue about himself. "I am often found in parks." He gives more clues, if necessary, becoming increasingly obvious until someone guesses correctly (in this case, a rubber ball).

For each round, other players introduce themselves in turn.

Variation:

Other items may be personified, such as zoo animals, home appliances, machines, etc.

Purpose or Benefit

"Personified Toy Box" encourages creativity, problem-solving reasoning, and puns.

Role Play

Number of Players:	4-12
Length of Time:	20-60 minutes
Materials:	A stack of 3x5 cards (or similar-sized pieces of paper) Pen or pencil Watch with a second hand
Preparation:	Situations which are to be acted out by one person are briefly described on the 3x5 cards. Appropriate situations would include ideas like "training a dog" or "riding in an elevator that gets stuck."
Object of the Game:	To effectively enact a role as assigned.

To Play:

Each participant takes a turn picking a card. In the one minute allotted, the player prepares to act out the situation described on his card. Following this time of preparation, he immediately begins to act out the assignment.

When the others guess what his situation is, he stops and another person takes a turn.

If, after three minutes, no one has successfully guessed, the actor stops and explains to the others what he was trying to portray.

Variations:

1. Situations may be designed for two or more people to perform together. In this case, the appropriate number of people chooses one card and decides together how they will act out the assignment.

2. A watch with a second hand may be used to keep track of how long it takes for the players to guess what the actor is doing.

3. Groups of people are assigned situations at the beginning of the activity. The groups then separate in order to discuss and rehearse their skits. When an agreed upon period of

time has passed (i.e., 10-20 minutes), each group returns and in turn performs its skit for the others.

4. Rather than being given situations, each group may be given a fruit of the Spirit (see Galatians 5:22-23). The groups then devise two skits: one with the fruit of the Spirit lacking, and the other with it present.

Purpose or Benefit

"Role Play" encourages creativity and imagination.

Scripture Skits

Number of Players: 6-25

Length of Time: 45-90 minutes

Object of the Game: To dramatize a Scripture passage.

To Play:

The players are divided into at least two teams (3-6 players per team), more if the group playing is large. Assign each group a Scripture passage.

Each team takes about 20 minutes to prepare a modern-day version of the passage/parable. After preparation, players return and perform the skits for each other.

Purpose or Benefit

"Scripture Skits" uses creative abilities, requires personal interaction, and can be humorous and upbuilding.

Word Charades

Number of Players: 4-20

Length of Time: 20-60 minutes

Object of the Game: To guess the word your team has been given to act out.

To Play:

The players are divided into two teams. One team leaves the room. Each team thinks of a list of words it wants the other team to act out by "charades" (pantomime). If the teams are not too large and there is enough time, it is good to choose the number of words equal to the number of players on each team.

For each word to be pantomimed, the team writes a word that *rhymes* with it on a separate slip of paper.

When the teams reunite, one of the rhyming words is revealed by one team to the opposing team. The opposing team then knows what the original word rhymes with, but does not know the original word. It is this team's task to guess the original word.

A player from the guessing team performs a pantomime of what he thinks the original word might be. If he is wrong, another team member attempts the same thing, and so on until the word is guessed or until they have made 10 attempts.

If the first player acts out the right word, his team is awarded 10 points. Each successive player has the chance to win his team one less point if he succeeds in acting out the word thought of by his opponents. The tenth attempt earns the team one point, if successful.

If the word is not guessed by the guessing team, the other team is awarded five points.

The next opportunity to guess a word is given to the other team. The teams alternate turns until all the rhyming clues are gone. The team with the highest total score wins.

Purpose or Benefit

"Word Charades" is a refreshing twist of the popular game of charades.

Your Radio Broadcast

Number of Players:	6-20
Length of Time:	60-90 minutes
Materials:	One cassette tape recorder for each group Blank tape for each group
Playing Site:	Large, comfortable room, and individual rooms for each group
Object of the Game:	For each group to record an original radio broadcast, including songs, interviews, commercials, features, etc.

To Play:

Participants are divided into groups of 3-6 people each. Each group is given a tape recorder and blank tape.

Each group is given about 30-40 minutes to put an original radio broadcast together on tape. The groups then all reassemble in a large room and play back their broadcasts to the other group(s).

Groups are free to be creative and innovative, using sports and newscasts, sound effects, panel discussions, foreign accents, commercials, background music, short stories, etc. Broadcasts may be secular or Christian, serious or humorous.

Variations:

1. Groups may *perform* their broadcasts for the others (rather than tape record them). In this case, props may be used, and possibly a makeshift Victrola set up behind which the players could "broadcast."

2. The entire group puts together one large radio broadcast, with individuals being assigned different roles and given 15-20 minutes each to prepare. In this case the broadcast is "live," and everyone is the audience. Individuals would thus come up and perform their role in the broadcast whenever the "announcer" called them.

Comments:

This activity will probably work best when people know each

other fairly well, and are aware of what types of roles one another could fit into best.

Purpose or Benefit

"Your Radio Broadcast" is very entertaining. It requires creativity, calls on people to work together, and is just as much fun to watch as it is to put together!

Musical Games

Create a Song

Number of Players:	6-30
Length of Time:	30-90 minutes
Materials:	Paper
	Pencils
Object of the Game:	To create an original song.

To Play:

The group is divided into two teams of equal size. More teams are formed if the group is large.

Each team goes into a separate room, and together the team members contribute to composing an original melody and lyrics for their song. No musical instruments may be used.

After a specified time limit, each team returns and sings their song for the others.

Variation:

Specific stipulations could be added, such as theme, length, or content.

Purpose or Benefit

"Create a Song" requires team effort and creativity. It provides an opportunity for small group relating within a larger group.

First-Liners

Number of Players:	3-20
Length of Time:	15-60 minutes
Object of the Game:	To come up with as many songs as possible having a specific word in their first lines.

To Play:

Players take turns singing first lines of songs containing a word chosen by the leader. For example, if the word chosen is "morning," one player could sing "Morning has broken"; the next, "Oh, what a beautiful morning," etc.

When a player has his turn and is unable to think of a song with that word, he is "out" for that round. The last player left "in" (i.e., always able to think of a first line) gets one point.

Players take turns choosing the word which must be present in each first line. When everyone has had a chance to choose the word (or, if the group is large, after a specified period of time), the person with the most points is the winner.

Variations:

There are many possible variations to this game:

1. The game can be played non-competitively, just for fun. Players take turns thinking of words. They go out when they cannot think of a song with the chosen word in it, but no points are accumulated and no winners identified.

2. Instead of a word, a theme or group of words can be chosen. For example, one theme could be "musical instruments" and the players have to sing the first line of any song that mentions one or more musical instrument (e.g., "76 Trombones," "MacNamara's Band," etc.). Or, a group of words could be anything to do with sun, sunny or sunshine. Themes and groups of words make the game a little easier to play for those who may not be familiar with a large number of songs.

3. Instead of "first lines," *any* line of a song containing the word can be sung.

4. "Alphabet First Liners": Instead of choosing a specific

138

word which has to occur in the first line, players go down the alphabet, and need to sing the first line of a song starting with the letter of the alphabet that they get.

5. "Word First-Liners": Instead of the alphabet, a certain word is chosen. The number of letters in the word should not equal or be a multiple of the number of people playing, to insure that the players do not always get the same letter. For example, if the word were "Sunshine," the first player would have to sing a first line starting with "S," the next player with "u," and so on.

6. After the first line is sung, the whole group attempts to sing the entire song together.

7. No special requirements are placed on the next first line to be sung, except that the player must not hesitate after the last player has finished.

8. Each player must sing the next line of the song started by the person before him.

Purpose or Benefit

"First-Liners" gets everyone singing and thinking of songs. It challenges the memory and familiarity with songs. This is a good game to play while waiting, or when on a long trip.

Hand-Clap Orchestra

Number of Players: 5-25

Length of Time: 15-45 minutes

Special Requirement: The leader must have a good sense of rhythm.

Object of the Game: To follow the leader and thus create a human orchestra of rhythms.

To Play:

The leader begins clapping rhythmically and asks the others to join in. The first clapping rhythm is quarter notes. He then changes the rhythm to half notes, and then eighth notes, so that the group understands the different values of the note.

He then divides the group into three sections and assigns one section to clap quarter notes, another half notes, and the other eighth notes.

He starts the orchestra by pointing to one section and beating out its notes with his hand. He changes the section he is pointing to as often as he wishes. Only the section he is pointing to at the moment claps. In this way, a musical pattern is created from the changes in note values.

After a while, the leader should rotate the notes to different sections to let the eighth note section rest and the half note section be more active.

Others may take turns at being the leader once they catch on.

Purpose or Benefit

"Hand-Clap Orchestra" promotes unity and group effort among participants. It may also serve to increase their sense of rhythm.

Limbo Dance

Number of Players:	5-30
Length of Time:	10-30 minutes
Materials:	Broomstick or other long, thin rod Recorded or live music (optional)
Physical Set-up:	Large open area
Preparation:	Music is started (if used).
Object of the Game:	To pass under the stick at a lower level than any other player.

To Play:

The broomstick is held horizontally at the height of the tallest player so that there is space for each player to pass under it.

The players form a line and walk under the broomstick, one at a time.

If the stick-holder wishes to participate, another player may replace him while he takes his turn.

After each player has had a turn, the stick is lowered slightly, and the players pass under it as before, leaning backwards, if necessary, to avoid touching the stick.

The stick is lowered again with each successive round.

To continue in the game, players must lean backwards to avoid the stick and may not touch the ground with any part of the body except the feet. Players who fail to do so are out of the game. Play continues until one player remains, who becomes the winner.

Purpose or Benefit

"Limbo Dance" is enjoyable to watch as well as to perform. It helps players develop balance and coordination.

Name That Tune

Number of Players:	5-20
Length of Time:	15-60 minutes
Materials:	A variety of music—either records or instrumental music A phonograph for records, or instrument and sheet music for musician Watch with a second hand
Object of the Game:	To guess the greatest number of song titles correctly.

To Play:

One person is in charge of playing the music. The players are divided into two teams of even numbers. Another person must keep time, or a player from each team can time the opposing team.

The length of time for the entire game should be decided before the game.

One person should keep score.

Music from a titled song is played (e.g., "Brahm's Lullaby" or "If I Were a Rich Man"). The whole song doesn't have to be played, just enough to allow it to be identified. After the music stops, one person from one of the two teams tries to name the tune correctly in a limited time. A good time limit is 15 seconds.

Teams alternate turns and the individuals on each team rotate turns.

If the player whose turn it is cannot name the tune, the opposing team has an equal amount of time to identify it. Any one player on the opposing team can try.

At the end of the allotted time, the team with the most points wins the game.

Variations:

1. A player from each team can compete at the same time to name the tunes the fastest.

2. Players can try to name tunes from a limited number of notes played.

Purpose or Benefit

"Name That Tune" draws on people's musical talent and knowledge, and can increase knowledge and interest in different types of music.

Orchestra

Number of Players:	3-15
Length of Time:	15-45 minutes
Materials:	Musical instruments Songbooks Pots and pans and other objects that make noise

Preparation: One player is appointed the conductor. The remaining players select instruments.

Object of the Game: To play music together as a makeshift orchestra.

To Play:

The conductor leads the group in playing a song from a songbook, or spontaneously. All play their instruments, trying to keep together rhythmically, without much concern for quality.

Comments:

"Orchestra" can begin as a group of people clear a table after a meal. As the dishes are being washed, someone (perhaps a guitarist) can lead the singing and assorted noise-making on kitchen utensils.

Consideration should be given to the fact that this kind of "orchestra" is very noisy.

Purpose or Benefit

Participants share in a creative and amusing activity.

Singing Commercials

Number of Players: 4-30

Length of Time: 30-90 minutes

Materials: Pencil and paper
Pictorial magazine ads

Object of the Game: To create a song to advertise the product in a picture.

To Play:

Participants are divided into two to six teams, each of which receives a pictorial magazine advertisement, pencil and paper.

The teams are instructed to create a song to promote the product in their picture. They are given a choice of three tunes to use. Catchy melodies known to all should be used, such as "A Bicycle Built for Two," "Tea for Two," or "Let Me Call You Sweetheart."

Each team meets separately to write original lyrics to the tune of their choice and to rehearse their performance of it.

The teams present their singing commercials to each other.

Variations:

1. The pictures are cut up like jigsaw puzzles so that each player can be given one piece. When the pieces are distributed, the players are instructed to find the rest of their picture. Thus, when everyone has found his picture, the teams are also formed around their pictures. Instructions for song writing are then given.

2. Instead of advertisements teams are given the actual products in paper bags.

3. Any melody may be used instead of giving limited choices.

Purpose or Benefit

Players interact in a lighthearted, creative game that provides humor and relaxes inhibitions.

Storytelling Games

Consequences

Number of Players:	2-12
Length of Time:	15-45 minutes
Materials:	Paper Pencils
Object of the Game:	To create humorous stories.

To Play:

Players are given paper and pencils. All pause for a few minutes to silently create their own story lines. Each story will be outlined as follows:
1. His name
2. Her name
3. Where they were
4. What they were doing
5. What he said
6. What she said
7. What the consequences were

Thus, an individual's story might read something like this: Adam (1) and Eve (2) were in the garden (3) eating some fruit (4). He said, "This is delicious!" (5) She said, "Aren't you glad you listened to me?" (6) The consequences were: They were cast out of the garden forever. (7)

When everyone is ready with a story, these narratives are recorded in the following manner: each player writes point #1 ("his name") at the top of his paper. Then he folds back the part he has written so that the writing can no longer be seen.

When all players have done this, they pass the papers once to the right. Each player will now have a new paper, and at the space at the top, he writes point #2, folding and passing it as before.

This procedure is repeated until all seven points have been recorded. When the last point has been written, players pass their papers one last time to the right.

Everyone may now read the paper in his possession, first to himself, then to the whole group. Since each story is actually a conglomeration of as many as seven original stories (depending on the number playing), the rearranged stories may be either simply nonsensical or thoroughly hilarious. If players wish, they may then reconstruct for one another their original stories. This game can be repeated many times.

The best stories are usually the products of original stories that were not necessarily wild or sensational. In fact, usually the "straighter" the originals are, the funnier the products will be.

The final stories will read more smoothly, however, if pronouns are used as much as possible after the initial introduction of the characters. Doing this will make the final stories sound more authentic.

Variations:

1. The following outline may be used in place of the one previously listed.
   a. This all happened to. . .

   b. It all began when . . .

   c. In a situation like this only one thing could happen. . .

   d. Suddenly, who should come along, but. . .

   e. And then the unexpected occurred. . .

   f. They both decided that. . .

   g. Our story draws to a close as. . .

These cues may be prewritten, in order, in fill-in-the-blank style, or a moderator may read them at the appropriate times.

2. "Literary Consequences" introduces an opportunity for artistic interpretation. Each player first writes the name of a book, then passes his paper. Under the title on his new paper, each player draws a picture to represent it. He then folds over only the writing to obscure it from the next player. After the papers are passed again, each player must write a book title that the picture could easily describe. After one more pass, the papers are exposed for the observation and amusement of all.

Purpose or Benefit

"Consequences" is a creative, yet simple, storytelling game that allows all to contribute to each accomplishment.

Continuous Story

Number of Players:	4-15
Length of Time:	20-45 minutes

Object of the Game: To create an interesting and complete story.

To Play:

One person in the group volunteers to start by making up and reciting the beginning of a story with a few (5-6) exciting sentences or a paragraph.

The person on his left continues the story, picking up where the first person left off. After telling another 4-5 sentences or so, he stops (perhaps even in mid-sentence) and lets the next person continue.

This continues until everyone has had a turn to contribute and the last person concludes the story with a happy ending, a lesson, or whatever he wants.

Variations:

1. Each person ends his turn by leaving the character in a predicament from which the next player has to "save" him.

2. Smaller groups give players more than one turn, to make the story longer.

3. The players decide before beginning on a particular type of story, e.g., humorous, serious, mystery, science fiction. If the story is to be humorous, the players should be cautioned against extreme silliness unless that is acceptable to the group.

Purpose or Benefit

This is a fun and entertaining way to interact and requires creativity and imagination. It is good to play with all ages, and new and old friends.

Fill-in-the-Blank Stories

Number of Players: 4-20

Length of Time: 20-60 minutes

Materials: A story or set of short stories (could

use paragraphs or short articles from newspapers, easy textbooks, history books, magazines, etc.). The stories should either be from material that can be marked in, or copies should be made of them.

Preparation: Stories are selected in advance and possibly copied.

Object of the Game: To create an interesting, funny story.

To Play:

One player is the leader for each story. The leader quickly reads through the story and crosses off a word or two in every sentence or two until there are about 10-20 blanks. Each word which is crossed off is labeled noun, verb, adjective, or whatever part of speech the word is.

Without announcing the title or topic of the story, the leader asks each player in the group, in turn, to supply one of the parts of speech crossed out. These new words are written in place of the old words until all blanks are filled in.

When all the old words have been replaced, the leader reads the story to the group.

Comments:

If each member of the group is eventually going to be the leader for creating a story, everyone could take a few minutes at the beginning to prepare his stories before beginning to play.

Purpose or Benefit

"Fill-in-the-Blank Stories" is a quiet, relaxing, humorous and creative game.

Fours

Number of Players: 3-30

Length of Time: 10-20 minutes

Materials: Paper
Pens or pencils

Object of the Game: To use the most four-letter words.

To Play:

Paper and pens or pencils are distributed to all. Participants each write a sentence using only words with four letters or less. Players score a point for each four-letter word used. If the same word is used more than once in a sentence, it counts as only one word. Players must stop writing at the end of a set time period, usually five to ten minutes.

All read their sentences and the player with the most points is the winner.

Variations:

1. Points are received for only five-letter words, or only six-letter words, etc.

2. The game can be repeated several times, with points for different numbers of letters each time. Points are accumulated each game to determine a winner at the end.

Purpose or Benefit

Players are challenged to quick thinking. Humor is provided when the sentences are read.

Rhyming Cards

Number of Players: 4-15

Length of Time: 30-60 minutes

Material: A deck of Rook ® cards

Object of the Game: To get rid of your cards and make up a rhyming poem.

To play:

The players sit in a circle or around a table and the cards are dealt two at a time until the deck is gone.

The person to the left of the dealer begins the game by laying down one card and saying a sentence about anything. The next person in the circle with the same number of another color lays his down and says a sentence that rhymes with, is rhythmically the same as, and makes some sense with the first sentence.

This goes around until all four of the same number cards are laid down and a four-line poem has been composed. The person laying down the fourth card then lays down another card and starts another poem. This goes on until all the cards are laid down.

The first player to run out of cards each time receives a point. The players continue until one player accumulates five points. The more people that play, the lower this number should be. The same rhyming word may not be used twice in the same poem.

Purpose or Benefit

An exercise in rhyming and quick thinking is provided in "Rhyming Cards."

Unending Sentence

Number of Players: 6-20

Length of Time: 5-30 minutes

Object of the Game: To add to a sentence without finishing it.

To Play:

A player begins a sentence with a short phrase. The other players each add a phrase to the sentence, trying not to end it.

If you end the sentence, you take the letter "O," the next time "U," and the next "T." When you spell OUT, you are out.

When a player gets a point, the next player starts a new sentence.

150

Example: 1st player says, The little girl . . .
2nd player says, The little girl with long brown hair . . .
and so on.

Comments:

It is fun to create crazy, long sentences.

Purpose or Benefit

This is an easy game that children and adults can play together. Players are challenged to alertness and creativity.

Why? Because!

Number of Players: 2-20

Length of Time: 15-30 minutes

Materials: Many small slips of paper
Pencils

Object of the Game: To create humorous questions and answers.

To Play:

Each player writes a designated number of "why" questions on slips of paper, with "because" answers on separate slips. All the "why" slips are placed in one container, and the "because" slips in another.

Players pass the containers around the room, taking turns drawing one "why" slip and one "because" slip, then reading the two together to form a question with its "logical" answer.

Sometimes the question-answers will be nonsense; other times the combination will be ironically humorous. Examples:
"Why did someone invent the light bulb? Because that's all there was to eat."
"Why did she serve us hamburger for dinner? Because he/she was experimenting with electricity."

Note: The person reading the question and answer can change

the pronouns, verb tenses, etc., to make the answer correspond to the question.

Variations:

1. Instead of "Why? Because," the format is changed to, "I like . . . because. . . ."

2. "Mixed-Up Similes": Each person writes a common simile such as "slow as a turtle," "naked as a jaybird," only putting the "slow as" on one slip of paper and "a turtle" on another, drawing them out of separate containers and reading them with humorous results.

Comments:

It is also fun to identify what was the original question-answer combination, the correct simile, or the original "I like . . . because . . ." statement after all the mixed-up combinations have been read.

Purpose or Benefit

"Why? Because!" is a noncompetitive game that is just for laughter and entertainment.

Word Whiskers

Number of Players:	4-20
Length of Time:	10-60 minutes
Materials:	A stopwatch or watch with a second hand Pencil Paper
Object of the Game:	To complete a 30-second monologue without using any word whiskers.

To Play:

Players are divided into two teams. One player serves as judge and scorekeeper. (This works well if an uneven number of players is present.) The judge gives a random topic to the first player or one of the teams (e.g., shoes, hair, traffic, elephants, anything!). The judge then begins timing for 30 seconds. The player attempts to talk about the assigned topic for 30 seconds without using any "word whiskers."

"Word whiskers" are filler words, such as "um," "er," "ya know," etc. If the player is successful, the judge scores a point for that team.

This player then gives a topic to the first player on the opposite team. The game continues until everyone on both teams has played.

Players may *not* begin their monologues using the *topic* as the first word. For instance, "Elephants are gray" would be disallowed. Instead, "One of the largest zoo animals is the *elephant*" would be an appropriate first sentence.

The speaker must not pause during his monologue for longer than 3 seconds. If he does, that is considered a word whisker also.

Purpose or Benefit

"Word Whiskers" requires concentration and encourages creativity. It can be very humorous.

RELATIONSHIP-BUILDING GAMES

These games focus on building relationships among the players by providing a way for them to get better acquainted and share positive input with each other. The sub-sections are:

> Getting-To-Know-Each-Other Games
> Games of Encouragement and Edification

Relationships can be built while playing almost any game; in these games, however, this is their special purpose.

Characteristic Hunt

Number of Players:	15-30
Length of Time:	15-45 minutes
Materials:	Paper and pencil for each person
Preparation:	A list of characteristics is compiled, to be matched with the people who are playing.
	They might include contact lenses, your color eyes, four children in his family, can recite John 3:16, is/was a business major, etc.
	These characteristics should be unusual unless planners *know* they fit specific people in the group.
	If desired, copies of the list may be reproduced for all the players.
Object of the Game:	To find people who fit each of the characteristics listed.

To Play:

Each player in the group receives a sheet of paper and pencil. Instructing the players to write the items in a column on their papers, the leader reads the list of characteristics (or the prepared copies are distributed).

Each person tries to find someone to match each characteristic on his sheet, and have it initialled by that person.

At the end of the game (a time limit may be set), the person with the most initialled characteristics wins.

Variation:

"Autograph Hunt": The players collect autographs of people whose *names* fit descriptions like: a famous queen, a name that rhymes with red, a biblical name, etc.

Purpose or Benefit

"Characteristic Hunt" helps people who do not know each other to get acquainted.

Do You Know Your Partner?

Number of Players:	5-21
Length of Time:	30-60 minutes
Materials:	Paper and pencil
Playing Site:	Facility where half the players may be separated so they cannot hear the other half
Preparation:	The moderator prepares a list of questions pertinent to all players. Four questions are sufficient for each round.
	Sample questions: (1) What would your partner do if he were given $5,000 and had three hours to spend it? (2) If your partner was offered a banana split, a hot fudge sundae, or apple pie, which would he choose? (3) What is your partner's favorite movie?
Object of the Game:	To correctly guess how one's partner will answer each question.

To Play:

Players are divided into pairs. One player serves as the moderator. One person from each pair leaves the room. The remaining players are then asked how they think their respective partners will answer each question. They answer aloud and then write each answer on paper.

The missing partners then return. Each is asked the questions previously asked of his partner. However, he answers for himself rather than his partner. A point is awarded for each response that matches how his partner said he would answer.

The other player from each couple then leaves the room, and the roles are reversed. The partnership with the most points at the end wins.

Variation:

If there are a large number of players, some can be spectators for one game (the "studio audience"), then play the next game while the original players watch.

Comments:

"Do You Know Your Partner?" can be played easily by people who hardly know each other, or those who know each other well.

Purpose or Benefit

This game helps people to get to know each other better and build closer relationships.

Have You Done This?

Number of Players:	5-25
Length of Time:	15-45 minutes
Object of the Game:	To make a statement about yourself that demonstrates your uniqueness among all those participating.

To Play:

Each player tries to think of a fact about himself that does not apply to any other player. When everyone is ready, each person takes a turn making his statement.

Examples could be, "I have never been to a movie," or "I have ten children."

The other players then indicate whether or not the statement is true for them. Play continues until everyone has made his statement.

Each player receives a point for each person who can also claim his statement. The person with the fewest points after one, or several games is the winner.

Purpose or Benefit

"Have You Done This?" challenges the imagination and gives players an opportunity to learn more about each other.

Life Story

Number of Players:	4-10
Length of Time:	45-90 minutes
Preparation:	One person is chosen in advance to give a brief oral autobiography. It is best for him to prepare the basic points he will cover. He may also bring photographs, a scrapbook, or other souvenirs of his past to show the group.
Object of the Game:	To learn more about each other.

To Play:

The person who is telling his life story shares some basic information: birth date, home town, family, etc., and continues sharing several important or unusual events that occurred in his life. Scrapbooks and pictures involve the audience and help them to visualize the experiences being recounted.

Purpose or Benefit

The group gets to know the speaker better and to have a greater appreciation for his experiences and personality. All enjoy hearing the often humorous anecdotes.

Personal Photographs

Number of Players:	5-15
Length of Time:	15-45 minutes
Materials:	A photograph of each person
Object of the Game:	To get to know each other better through seeing a picture and listening to a story.

To Play:

Each person brings a photograph of himself, preferably of an early age.

Each player thinks of a significant or funny event related to the picture or period of life the picture represents.

The first person begins by passing the photograph he brought around the group. As it goes around, he shares a significant or funny event in his life (for about two to three minutes).

The rest of the players listen respectfully while he talks. They can ask questions or make comments when he is finished.

Each player takes his turn passing his photograph and relating his story.

Variation:

Each player brings a baby or early childhood picture of himself. The leader of the game has all the photos. He passes one around the group. Then each member of the group guesses who the person is. The person may then talk about an event related to the photo.

Purpose or Benefit

"Personal Photographs" encourages listening and personal exposure. It is a good vehicle to build personal relationships among participants.

Personal Trivia

Number of Players:	4-15
Length of Time:	20-90 minutes
Materials:	Paper and pencils Small bowl or bag
Object of the Game:	To guess which player is described by the facts presented.

To Play:

Each player briefly writes down three facts/events/experiences from his life that he hopes are unknown to anyone else in the group. It is best to have a set time limit for the procedure (recommended: 5-10 minutes).

The papers are folded and collected in the bowl or bag.

One person reaches in for a paper and reads through the three facts twice. Either a designated leader can read it, or turns can be taken.

The player to the reader's right begins the guessing and it continues until everyone has named someone he thinks is described by the facts.

The correct person reveals himself and then has the option to elaborate on his facts.

The first person who guessed correctly picks the next paper from the bowl.

Variations:

1. Limitations on facts can be set (e.g., in high school, on vacations), or married couples may write three upbuilding facts about their spouses.

2. To prevent the players from identifying the last sets of facts by elimination, all the papers are read before any guessing is done. In this case, it is best for players to number and record their choices on paper.

3. A point is scored for each correct guess, to eventually determine a winner with the highest score.

4. It may be desirable to have each player submit *more* than

three facts/events/experiences from his life on a piece of paper.

Comments:

The game is best played among people that are at least somewhat acquainted with one another.

Players should be encouraged to elaborate on their facts orally at the appropriate times in the game.

Purpose or Benefit

"Personal Trivia" allows players to get to know each other in ways not possible in normal conversation.

Questions

Number of Players:	5-15
Length of Time:	30-60 minutes
Object of the Game:	To get to know individuals in the group better by listening.

To Play:

Each person in the group gets a chance to be the "responder." The group asks the responder questions for him to answer on any subject (e.g., childhood, opinions on a subject, his likes or dislikes, etc.). The group should use creativity to think of interesting questions.

Variations:

1. Instead of going around the room and asking questions verbally to individuals, everyone prepares questions he would like to ask *anyone* in the room and writes them on slips of paper. These are put in a bowl which is passed around the room. Each person takes turns drawing a question and responding to it while everyone listens. When the responder has finished answering he passes the bowl to the next person.

2. Others in the group may address questions or comments to

the individuals responding, either: (1) after the person has finished responding, before the next person begins, or (2) at the time of their turn (have paper and pencil available for each person to write down any comments or questions until his turn comes).

Purpose or Benefit

"Questions" exercises listening abilities. Many interesting things can be learned about those in the group.

Games of Encouragement and Edification

Appreciation Bookmarks

Number of Players:	2-15
Length of Time:	45-90 minutes
Materials:	Colored construction paper Scissors Glue Clear contact paper Pens and felt markers Bibles
Playing Site:	Room large enough so that each player has ample space in which to write, draw, cut, etc. A large table is ideal, but not necessary.
Object of the Game:	To make clear, plastic-coated encouraging bookmarks for each person.

To Play:

Each person is given a piece of construction paper and pen(s). Scissors, glue, and Bibles can be shared among several players.

Players take time to think, prayerfully perhaps, of some quality or characteristic which they appreciate in each of the other players. If the group is larger than eight, then names should be drawn so that each person thinks of a quality for eight of the other players.

For each (or eight) of the other players, each player writes the trait he has thought of on a small section of colored paper (in a few upbuilding words) and cuts it out. For example: "Mary, you are a patient, understanding mother to your children, and an example to me," or, "What I like about you, John, is your consistent cheerfulness and great sense of humor."

Each person will construct a bookmark for the person on his right. He should collect all the slips of paper written for that person. He should also select a Scripture passage which would be meaningful, or especially suited for that person, and write it on a piece of construction paper, or on the bookmark itself.

When the player has collected all of the papers which were written for the person on his right, he arranges them with the Scripture verse on a piece of construction paper cut to be the size of a bookmark. He then finishes constructing the bookmark by gluing all the slips of paper on the construction paper and cutting the contact paper to make a contact covering (of the same size) for the bookmark.

When all the bookmarks are finished, each person takes turns reading aloud the bookmark he made for the person on his right and presents it to him.

Variations:

1. "Do it yourself" laminating kits are available in stores and can be used instead of contact paper. If this is done, an iron is necessary.

2. The bookmarks may be further decorated with small pictures, designs, etc., before the contact paper is added.

Comments:

This is more of a serious activity than a "game," but is very enjoyable. It should be done in a joyful, loving atmosphere.

Players should write as neatly as they can to add to the attractiveness and positive effects of the finished products.

Purpose or Benefit

"Appreciation Bookmarks" is a great way to edify and

strengthen one another in the truth. It also produces a *tangible* reminder for each player of how God has worked in his life and how he is liked and appreciated by his brothers and sisters.

Attribute Attributers

Number of Players: 4-15

Length of Time: 1-2 hours

Materials: Pencil and paper for the leader of the game

Playing Site: An extra room is needed where one player can go while the others consult

Special Requirement: It is helpful if the persons playing the game know each other fairly well, at least well enough that each player could think of an attribute or character quality of each other player.

Object of the Game: To identify who attributed an attribute to you. To edify and encourage one another by expressing to them the qualities and attributes you appreciate in them.

To Play:

One player leaves the room. Each of the other players thinks of an attribute he likes about him. The leader writes down the attributes, with the name of the person who contributed each one next to it.

The absent player returns and the leader reads the attributes to him one at a time. The absent player tries to identify who attributed each attribute to him. He scores a point for each correct guess.

The first person correctly identified is the next person to leave the room.

Each player is given his list of attributes to keep.

Comments:

If the group is large and time is taken for each player to leave
the room, it could take a long time. A time limit may be set,
and only the number of players who can leave the room during
the time limit will be able to do so.

Purpose or Benefit

"Attribute Attributers" builds relationships and encourages
and edifies the players.

Building Ties

Number of Players:	6-15
Length of Time:	30-60 minutes
Material:	One ball of yarn that contains approximately eight feet of yarn per player
Object of the Game:	To encourage each other with positive statements; to build interpersonal ties.

To Play:

Participants should take a few minutes to think about each
person in the game and to bring to mind things that they like
or admire about that person.

All players are seated. One person takes the ball of yarn and
tells another person something he likes or admires about that
person. Then, holding onto the end of the string, he throws the
ball to the person to whom he spoke.

That person in turn follows the same procedure, and so on, until all persons have had at least one turn. The game can last as
long as the string holds out. Then it reverses order, winding
the ball up again.

Purpose or Benefit

"Building Ties" increases self-esteem and gives participants
feedback on how others see them.

Honoring Chair

Number of Players: 4-10

Length of Time   45-90 minutes

Materials: Paper
                        Pencils

Object of the Game: To verbally honor and encourage one
                        another.

To Play:

To begin, each person participating in this activity writes a
short comment concerning every other person participating.
These comments should be written with the object of honoring
the person whom they are writing about.

For example: "I feel you have a servant's heart, eager to help
others, and your example has inspired me to serve more cheer-
fully."

When everyone has finished writing, one person is chosen to
sit in a chair in the center of the room. The rest of the people
then each take a turn sharing the comment they wrote which
pertains to the person sitting in the chair. When all have
shared, another person takes the chair and all share the comments they wrote concerning him. This continues until each
has had a seat in the chair and has heard what the others had
written concerning him.

Variation:

The comments may be prepared several days in advance, in
which case they need not be quite as brief and will be somewhat better thought out.

Comments:

It is often helpful to pray before writing comments to build up
one another. Comments need to be considered deeply and not
be shallow or repetitive.

Purpose or Benefit

"Honoring Chair" will increase the participants' appreciation
for one another as well as improving each individual's self-
esteem.

Strength Identification

Number of Players:	5-15
Length of Time:	20-60 minutes
Materials:	Paper
	Pencil
	Bowl or bag
Special Requirement:	The players need to be somewhat acquainted with each other
Object of the Game:	To guess the person that a list of strengths describes, and the author of the list.

To Play:

The name of each player is written on a piece of paper; the papers are folded and collected in the bowl or bag by the leader.

Each player draws a piece of paper with the name of another player on it. Thinking about the person drawn, each then lists three to six strengths of character or positive attributes of the person on the same paper. The author signs his own name on the bottom. The papers are refolded and collected in the bowl or bag.

The leader draws a paper from the bowl/bag and reads just the strengths listed, leaving out both names. After each player tries to guess who was being described, the leader reveals his identity.

The players then try to identify the author; the author is also revealed. This process is repeated as the leader goes through all the papers.

Each person described can keep the list of his strengths for his own encouragement.

Comments:

"Strength Identification" works best when the players know each other fairly well. It is good for people who get together regularly for fellowship, and families where strengths are observed daily.

Purpose or Benefit

"Strength Identification" facilitates getting to know the other players better and points out the Christlike character in each player.

GUESSING GAMES

Guessing games are popular, and they come in many different forms. We have grouped them in four categories:

Games in Which One Person Guesses
Making the Others Guess
Guessing Disguised Subjects
Miscellaneous Guessing Games

Many of these games are popular *children's* games. Others are very challenging to *adults*, especially those where disguised subjects are guessed. Many of the guessing games will be enjoyed by adults and children alike.

Applause

Number of Players: 3-30

Length of Time: 15-90 minutes

Object of the Game: To get the person who has left the
                       room to accomplish a specified ac-
                       tion.

To Play:

While one person is out of the room, the others decide what he
should do when he returns (e.g., place an object in a certain
place, shake each person's hand, etc.).

When the person returns, the others begin to clap slowly. As
the person more closely approximates the planned activity,
they clap more quickly; as he is getting farther from it, they
clap more slowly. If he is using the right object, but doing the
wrong thing with it, they speed up their clapping and slow
down quickly until he gets closer to doing the right thing.

When the person succeeds in doing the activity, another person leaves the room, and the game continues.

Variations:

1. An object is hidden in the room, which the person must
   find.

2. One or all players tap pie tins with spoons instead of clapping.

3. Players slap their laps instead of clapping.

Comments:

It may help to have someone who has played before leave the
room first, as an example of how to figure out what to do.

This must be approached properly or it can make the person
who is "it" feel he/she is being laughed at. It should be
stressed that the applause is encouragement.

In situations where the noise level must be kept low, players

170

may raise their hands and wave them when the person approximates the right thing. When the person succeeds at the final activity, all players stand.

Purpose or Benefit

"Applause" stimulates creativity. It can be played easily by children, or children and adults together.

At the Stick's End

Number of Players:	4-12
Length of Time:	10-30 minutes
Materials:	Blindfold Stick or pole five to six feet long
Object of the Game:	For the person in the middle: to guess which player has grabbed the end of his stick. For the other players: to disguise their voices so as not to be guessed.

To Play:

One player is blindfolded, placed in the center of the circle that the other players have formed, and holds the stick in his hand. The other players dance around him in a circle until he stretches out his stick and points it. At this time they must stop and "freeze" and the person that the stick is pointing to, or nearest to the stick, must grab the end of it.

The person in the middle asks the person who has grabbed it a question. The "grabber" answers, disguising his voice so as not to be guessed. The players can make up their own questions and answers, or the following rhymes can be chanted:

The "pointer" asks, "Who did I pick, who did I pick, who did I pick at the end of my stick?" To which the "grabber" can call out in a disguised voice, this rhyme, "I won't tell, I won't tell, I won't tell if you make me yell!"

The pointer has one chance to guess who is behind the disguised voice. If he succeeds, the "grabber" becomes the blind-folded pointer in the middle, and they exchange places. If he fails, he must repeat the original procedure.

Variations:

1. "Fisherman Game": One person stands in the middle, blindfolded, with the others in a circle around him. He holds a stick or pole with a long string attached to it as a fishing pole. The other players move around him in a circle, and he "casts" his line out into the circle. Whoever the string comes closest to catches it and tugs on it. The fisher-man has three guesses to identify who has "caught" his bait.

2. A variation of the "Fisherman Game" is that each player takes the name of a fish (e.g., "Perch," "Northern," "Trout," etc.). The fisherman then guesses what kind of fish he has caught. The fisherman is not necessarily blind-folded.

Comments:

This game is suitable for ages 4-12. Some four-year-olds may not be able to disguise their voices or like to be blindfolded; therefore the "Fisherman Game" may be better for them. Boys especially enjoy this game.

Purpose or Benefit

"At the Stick's End" is a creative, moderately active chil-dren's game. It provides physical activity, but keeps it lim-ited.

The Common Word

Number of Players:	4-12
Length of Time:	15-60 minutes
Playing Site:	An extra room is needed where one player can go while the others consult
Object of the Game:	For the players who have determined

the common word together: to disguise the word in their answers so it cannot be discerned by the investigator. For the investigator: to discern the common word that has been agreed upon.

To Play:

One player is designated the "investigator" and leaves the room. The remaining players consult and agree on what is to be the common word.

The investigator returns and is allowed to ask a question of each player. Each player must give an answer of three medium-length sentences or less and use the common word in his answer.

The investigator can at any time make a guess as to the common word. He is allowed five guesses.

If the investigator is correct on his first guess, he receives 5 points, on his second guess 4, and on his third 3, etc. One person keeps score.

Variation:

To make the game more difficult, the players must answer the investigator's question with only one medium-length sentence using the common word.

Purpose or Benefit

"The Common Word" requires creativity in thinking of an answer that will disguise a common word, yet adequately answers the question.

Doggie, Doggie, Where's Your Bone?

Number of Players:	4-15
Length of Time:	10-30 minutes
Materials:	Chair
	Object to represent a doggie bone

Object of the Game: For the doggie to guess who has taken the bone.

To Play:

The person appointed as the first "doggie" sits in the chair and looks straight ahead. The "bone" is placed close behind him. The other players are all behind the chair, a few steps away from the bone.

One person sneaks up and takes the bone. He returns to his previous position and hides the bone behind his back. All players except the doggie chant, "Doggie, doggie, where's your bone? Cops and robbers took it home."

The doggie then gets three guesses as to who took his bone (or only one if the group is small). If doggie guesses wrong, he remains the doggie for the next game. If he guesses right, the robber becomes the new doggie.

Purpose or Benefit

"Doggie, Doggie, Where's Your Bone?" can be enjoyed by children as young as four years old.

Find the Leader

Number of Players: 5-25

Length of Time: 20-30 minutes

Object of the Game: To guess who is directing the group to change from one motion to another.

To Play:

One person is chosen to be "it," and is sent out of the room. One of the people left is chosen to be the leader.

The leader of the group directs the group in some kind of simple motion (e.g., hand-clapping, thumb-twiddling, whistling, tongue-clicking, etc.). All others in the group imitate the leader so everyone is doing the same thing, *together*.

"It" is called back into the room and stands in the middle of the circle the others have formed. The leader changes the motion repeatedly. He and the others in the circle try to keep together, so that the leader is inconspicuous.

As the group goes through the pattern of motions, "it" tries to guess who the leader is. "It" gets only three guesses. If "it" doesn't "Find the Leader," he is "it" again (maximum of two times to be "it"). The leader always becomes the next "it."

Comments:

This game is most effective when played for shorter periods of time.

Purpose or Benefit

"Find the Leader" shows the importance of cooperation and togetherness. This is a good game for children as well as adults.

Hidden Sentences

Number of Players:	4-12
Length of Time:	30 minutes to 2 hours
Materials:	Paper Pencils
Playing Site:	Two chairs, facing each other in a large room
Object of the Game:	To use a hidden sentence without it being detected, and to detect the opponent's hidden sentence.

To Play:

Players divide into two teams. One person from each team then leaves the room. The two teams separate and each team writes an "unlikely" sentence to be the hidden sentence for the player from the opposing team who has left the room. An example might be, "If cars grew wings when going south, birds would fly north in the fall."

The two players who have left the room are then asked back in and each team gives its sentence to the player from the opposing team. The two players, after having read their assigned sentences, then sit in the two chairs facing one another and enter into a conversation.

As they talk each player attempts to state his sentence in a natural way without the other player detecting it. At the same time, each player attempts to detect the other player's hidden sentence. The conversation may be interrupted at any time if a player guesses that something the other player just said was his hidden sentence. However, only three guesses are allowed.

Scoring: If a player correctly guesses his opponent's hidden sentence, his team receives two points. If a player successfully states his hidden sentence without his opponent detecting it, his team receives two points. If a player guesses three times incorrectly, then the opposing team is awarded one point.

When the play is completed, points are awarded and a new player from each team leaves the room. The teams then write new sentences and the game continues. When all members of each team have had their turn with a hidden sentence, the final score is totalled and the team with the greatest number of points is the winner.

Variation:

"Silly Story": Instead of having the two players face one another and engage in a conversation, they are required to each separately tell a story, in which the sentence is hidden, to one another. The resulting stories are usually ridiculous and highly entertaining. Scoring procedure remains the same as that in "Hidden Sentences."

Comments:

Players watching the two players who are having the conversation must be careful not to give any hints or disclose information through inadvertent facial expressions or gestures.

Purpose or Benefit

This game demands a lot of creativity and quick thinking—as well as some acting ability. There is much fun interaction as well as challenge in this game.

Mystery Shadow

Number of Players:	4-15
Length of Time:	15-45 minutes
Materials:	A large sheet A lamp A chair
Playing Site:	A large sheet is hung at one end of the room with enough space to walk behind without being detected. In front of a doorway is ideal, or in a hallway. A lamp is set on a table behind the sheet and a chair placed a good distance in front of it.
Preparation:	The leader of the game prepares the sheet, lamp and chair as prescribed above.
	The leader should test the visual effects of the lamp behind the sheet before the game is to begin.
Object of the Game:	For the detective to guess the identity of the figures behind the sheet. For the players to conceal their identity.

To Play:

One player is chosen to be the "detective." He is seated on the chair in front of the sheet. The other players take turns walking behind the sheet. The light behind the sheet creates a blurred shadow effect on their forms. They try to conceal their identity by walking (or crawling or dancing) in unusual ways, making facial expressions or other distorted movements.

The detective calls out names for each shadow. When he successfully identifies someone, that person becomes the detective.

Comments:

If there is no available doorway, hallway, or other place to hang the sheet so that the entrance and exit of the players walking behind it are concealed, large blankets can be hung at both ends of the sheet. The players can then stand behind them to be hidden from the detective's sight.

Purpose or Benefit

People of just about any age can play and enjoy "Mystery Shadow."

Who Are You?

Number of Players: 5-12

Length of Time: 30-90 minutes

Object of the Game: To communicate or guess who the famous person is.

To Play:

One player leaves the room while others decide on a famous person that the player will "be" when he returns. They also decide on a situation to dramatize in order to help the player guess who he is (e.g., if the player is to be Lafayette, they could enact a general staff meeting and advise him on his next battle).

When the player who left the room comes back, the rest of the players enact the situation they planned, relating to the player as if he were the famous person. They continue until the player guesses who he is.

The procedure is repeated with the other players.

Purpose or Benefit

Participants are encouraged to interact and be creative.

Botticelli

Number of Players: 3-15

Length of Time: 20-90 minutes

Object of the Game: To guess the name of the person or character selected by "it."

To Play:

One person is "it." He must silently think of the name of a person *or* fictitious character. This character is referred to by the initial of his last name (e.g. "Mr. F.").

The players, in turn, ask "it" yes-or-no questions in order to discover the name of "it's" character. However, they must earn the opportunity to ask each question by asking "it" to name a character with the same initial in response to their questions. For example, "it" begins play with the statement, "I am thinking of a Mr. B." A player then asks "it" a question such as, "Was Mr. B a president?" If "it" cannot name a president whose name starts with B, the player has earned the right to ask "it" *one* yes-no question in order to obtain clues regarding the character's identity. However, if "it" is able to name a Mr. B who was a president (regardless of whether or not it is the same person the player had in mind), that player forfeits the opportunity to question "it." The player who correctly guesses the name of "it's" character is the new "it."

Variations:

1. "Free" questions may be asked, rather than limiting them to ones with yes or no answers.

2. It may be advisable to set a time limit (15-30 seconds is good) on how long "it" can take to respond.

3. The selection is limited to a category of names, such as Bible characters, inventors, artists, etc.

4. In small groups, players may ask questions as they think of them, rather than asking in turn.

5. The game is made more difficult if questions are limited by knowledge gained from previous answers. For example, one could not try to stump "it" by asking "Are you a comic-strip character?" if he already knew that the character was real.

Purpose or Benefit

"Botticelli" is intellectually stimulating and requires creative thinking, yet can be played by children and adults alike.

I Spy

Number of Players: 2-12

Length of Time: 5-30 minutes

Object of the Game: To guess correctly the object described.

To Play:

Players take turns being the "spy." The spy scans the room with his eyes until he finds an object he wants the others to guess. He describes it by saying, "I spy something (*adjective*)." He could say red, striped, dull, pointed, or fuzzy—any one adjective that gives a clue.

The others try to guess what the spy described. If they are stumped, the spy can give them additional clues of the same kind until someone guesses correctly. The person who guesses correctly is the next spy.

Variation:

The spy reveals the first letter of the object to be identified. In this version, the spy says, "I spy something beginning with ———."

Purpose or Benefit

Players are challenged to use perception and imagination.

People Puzzler

Number of Players:	3-20
Length of Time:	30-90 minutes
Materials:	Paper Pencils Set of encyclopedias
Object of the Game:	To identify the famous person and stump the other players.

To Play:

Each player is given one volume of the encyclopedia along with paper and pencil.

One player is designated the leader. At a signal from the leader each player, including the leader, looks through his volume of the encyclopedia to find three facts relating to a famous person. This famous person can be either real or imaginary. Each player then writes the three facts he has found or made up and waits quietly for the other players to finish.

When all players have finished writing, the leader indicates one player who reads aloud the three facts he has written without revealing the identity of the famous person to whom the facts relate. The rest of the players then proceed to guess who the famous person is or whether the facts relate to an imaginary person. As each player guesses, the player who read the facts silently keeps tally of the score, according to the scoring procedures outlined below. After everyone has made a guess, the player who read reveals the identity of the famous person and awards each player his points.

The leader then indicates another player who reads his three facts aloud. The game continues until all have had a chance to read their facts and have the group guess the identity of their famous person. In the final tally of points, the player who scores highest is the winner.

Scoring: the player who reads his facts is awarded two points each time one of the players who is guessing makes a wrong guess at the identity of his famous person. A player who makes a correct guess and names the famous person is awarded five points. A player who correctly guesses that the famous person is imaginary is awarded three points.

Variation:

Any topic, other than famous people, may be used in this game. For example, famous cities, or animals, or sports would be acceptable.

Purpose or Benefit

"People Puzzler" provides a creative challenge to try to stump the other players.

Scripture Detective

Number of Players:	4-12
Length of Time:	15-60 Minutes
Materials:	A Bible for each person
Object of the Game:	To find the chapter and verse of each Bible event referred to.

To Play:

Each player locates several incidents of Scripture (e.g., Moses parting the Red Sea) and writes down the book, chapter, and verse from which each came.

Each person takes a turn as moderator and chooses one of the incidents of Scripture that he himself has written. After stating the event (or text of the verse), the other players search for the exact book, chapter, and verse where it is found.

The first person to discover the location must raise his hand and await recognition by the moderator. When the moderator gives permission, the player may give his answer. If his answer is correct, he is awarded two points; if he is wrong, he is penalized one point.

The role of moderator rotates to the next player after each search. At the end of the final rotation, the player with the most points wins.

Comments:

Care should be taken not to choose events from Scripture that are retold in other books. Similar Bible translations should be used.

Purpose or Benefit

Greater familiarity with the Bible is gained through playing "Scripture Detective."

Twenty Questions

Number of Players:	2-20
Length of Time:	20-90 minutes
Materials:	Pencil Paper
Preparation:	The group is divided into two teams. Each person should have a piece of paper and a pencil, or each team can designate one person to keep score.
Object of the Game:	To guess the person, place, or thing correctly in the least number of questions.

To Play:

One team agrees among themselves about a person, place or thing for the other team to guess. Members of the other team take turns asking yes or no questions of the first team until they guess correctly, or use up all of their quota of 20 questions. They receive a point for each question asked.

The first team then has a turn to ask questions about something the other team as agreed on. The team with the fewest points wins.

Variations:

1. Each team takes three turns, accumulating points toward a final score. Teammates confer at the beginning of the game as to what their three subjects will be.

2. Instead of dividing into teams, one person thinks of something and the rest of the group asks the questions.

3. The subject to be guessed may be animal, vegetable, or mineral. Players can ask which it is as part of their questioning.

4. The team asking questions can talk or strategize while asking questions.

5. The team asking questions has only one minute to ask a question. If no question is asked during the one minute, then it counts as a question.

6. For adults or older children, abstract, imaginary, or invisible "things" can be chosen for the other team to guess (e.g., heat, cold, youth, spirit). More than 20 questions may be allowed if the number of questions is agreed upon by all before the game begins.

Purpose or Benefit

"Twenty Questions" stimulates curiosity, logical thinking, and encourages patience.

Twenty Questions by Teams

(A Variation for Large Groups)

Number of Players:	12-40
Length of Time:	30-60 minutes
Playing Site:	Large room of sufficient area for teams to be spaced a fair distance apart
Object of the Game:	To guess the subjects selected by all the other teams, by asking as few questions as possible.

To Play:

Choose a leader. The leader divides the group into equal teams. Four to six people per team is a good size. Each team takes the name of a country. Each team decides on a subject.

Each team then sends out an "ambassador" who will go around and be asked 15 questions by each team about his team's subject. The leader directs the movement of the ambassadors from country to country. It is helpful if the teams are arranged in a circle around the room. This way the leader can say, "All ambassadors go to the next country on their right," every few minutes. This keeps them moving to each team in an orderly fashion, so that only one ambassador is visiting each team at a time.

The 15 questions asked of the ambassador may be only "yes" or "no" questions. It is helpful to have one person on each team be a secretary who writes the name of each country and the answers to the questions asked of that country's ambassador.

After each ambassador has returned to his team, each team tries to guess what the other teams' subjects were. If after 15 questions any team is prepared to guess the subjects of the other countries, it announces its guesses. For each correct guess the team receives 10 points. For each incorrect guess the team is penalized three points.

If not all the subjects have been correctly guessed, ambassadors are sent out again from the remaining teams and are asked five more questions. After they return, teams may again make their guesses. At this point a team gets five points for each correct guess, and is penalized two points for each incorrect guess.

If all teams' subjects are not correctly identified at this point, ambassadors again are sent out from the remaining teams and asked five more questions by each team. At this point the teams receive three points for each correct guess and are penalized one point for each incorrect guess.

Ambassadors may be sent out only one more time if necessary. The same scoring as in the previous paragraph applies. If at this time a team's subject has still not been identified by any of the other teams, it receives a special bonus of 10 points.

Variation:

To make the game easier and quicker, the subjects can be limited to either a person, place or thing. In this case, instead of starting with 15 questions, it is better to start with 10.

Purpose or Benefit

"Twenty Questions by Teams" can be played by a large number of people and encourages cooperation in arriving at questions and answers.

What's My Line?

Number of Players:	6-20
Length of Time:	45-90 minutes
Materials:	Pencils Small pieces of paper
Object of the Game:	To guess an occupation in the least possible number of guesses.

To Play:

The group is divided into two teams of equal size. The teams go to separate rooms and confer among themselves. They write the name of a different occupation on each piece of paper, one for each member of the opposing team.

After the teams come back together a person from one team draws a paper that the other team has written. His team members ask him yes-or-no questions until they guess the occupation, receiving a point for each question asked.

The teams take turns drawing papers from each other, selecting a different team member each time, until all the papers have been used. The team with the lowest score wins.

Variations:

1. One person prepares the subjects to be guessed ahead of time, and people from the group at large take turns drawing them instead of forming teams. Scores are earned individually, or no scores are kept.

2. Instead of determining the occupation through questions answered, the person who draws the occupation panto-

mimes it. The length of time or number of guesses it takes his team to identify it is tallied. The team with the lowest time or number wins.

3. The game can be played with a larger group of people divided into more than two teams.

Purpose or Benefit

"What's My Line?" encourages curiosity, logic and patience.

Guessing Disguised Subjects

The Dictionary Game

Number of Players:	3-12
Length of Time:	1-2 hours
Materials:	Dictionary Several sheets of paper for each player Pens or Pencils for each player Hard surfaces to write on
Object of the Game:	To accumulate the most points by:

1. Creating definitions that other players will think are from the dictionary.

2. Correctly guessing the real definitions of words among several false ones.

To Play:

Paper and pencils are distributed to all. One person has the dictionary.

The person chooses a word from the dictionary he thinks no one knows. He asks if anyone knows what the word means; if anyone does, he chooses another word. After an unfamiliar word is found, each player writes an imaginary definition for the word, then passes his paper to the person with the dictionary.

The person with the dictionary writes an imaginary definition as well as copying the real definition onto a separate sheet of paper.

The person with the dictionary reads each definition silently. This is important so that his tone of voice, difficulty in pronouncing words, or outbursts of laughter do not reveal which definitions are imaginary. He then mixes the papers up, and reads each definition aloud.

As the person with the dictionary reads them aloud a second time,* the others vote by raising their hands for the definition they think is the real one. (It is best to have all players decide before anyone votes, to minimize their influence on each other.) When all have voted, the person with the dictionary reveals the real definition and then other players may reveal which ones they wrote.

Each player scores 1 point for every vote his definition receives and 3 points if he has voted for the real definition.

The dictionary is passed to another person, and the procedure is repeated.

There is no specific way to end the game, except as decided by those playing.

Variation:

If there is a large number of players, the group can be divided into teams. This may be a good alternative if a faster-paced game is desired.

Each member of the team which submits the word makes up a false definition for it. The individual members of the other team(s) guess which definition is correct.

The team submitting the word scores one point each time a false definition receives a vote.

A team scores three points each time one of its members selects the correct definition.

Purpose or Benefit

"The Dictionary Game" encourages and challenges the players' creativity. It also allows players to enjoy and learn more about each other.

―――――

*Additional readings may be necessary with larger groups because there will be more definitions to remember.

Guess the Product

Number of Players: 4-15

Length of Time: 20-60 minutes

Materials: Paper and pencil for each player

Preparation: The leader prepares in advance a list of products with their definitions and categories. The number of products depends on how long the game is to be.

 Examples:
  Category—laundry detergent
  Definition—a shout of approval
  Product—Cheer

  Category—soap
  Definition—hearty enjoyment; gusto
  Product—Zest

  Category—cars
  Definition—a wild horse
  Product—Mustang

Object of the Game: To name the product corresponding to its category and definition.

To Play:

The leader reads several categories and definitions, which each player writes down. The players each try to produce the right answers in 5-10 minutes.

At the end of the round the leader reads the correct answers and each player scores one point for each correct answer. The person with the most points wins.

Variations:

1. For a longer game, a number of people could prepare a list of products in advance so each could lead a round of play.

2. "Guess the Product" could be played two ways by teams:

   a. Each team makes a list of products, categories and definitions for the other team to guess within a time limit.

   b. The leader states the category and definition and the first team to call out the answer gets the point.

Purpose or Benefit

"Guess the Product" challenges the players to quick thinking and creativity.

Headline Summaries

Number of Players:	5-10
Length of Time:	10-20 minutes
Materials:	Pencil and paper for each player A compiled list of "summaries" and answers
Preparation:	The leader prepares a list of one-line summaries of stories or rhymes (e.g., "Child frightened by a spider," for "Little Miss Muffet").
Object of the Game:	To guess the rhyme or story suggested by each headline summary.

To Play:

The leader reads the summaries to the contestants; the first person to guess the title of the story or rhyme earns a point.

The person with the most points at the end of the game wins.

Variation:

Bible quotes and stories can be used as subject matter, as can famous incidents in history.

Purpose or Benefit

Quick thinking for placing headlines with topics is developed. Imagination is stimulated in creating summaries.

Hidden Sayings

Number of Players:	3-14
Length of Time:	10-30 minutes
Materials:	Paper, pencils for each player
Preparation:	"Hidden Sayings" can be played by individuals or by teams. If it is played by individuals, the leader of the game needs to prepare a list of hidden sayings. If it is played by teams, the leader simply divides the group into equal teams, and gives pencil and paper to each team.
Object of the Game:	To find the hidden sayings.

To Play:

The leader of the game gives each player a copy of a list of famous/popular sayings, proverbs or maxims, which have been written in such a way that they are difficult to identify.

For example, the saying, "The early bird catches the worm," could be written as, "THEE ARL YBI RDCA TCHE STH EWO RM."

When played by individuals, each player is given a list and a time limit in which to decipher as many sayings as he can. The person who has deciphered the most in the time limit is the winner.

When played by teams, each team produces a list of sayings for the opponents. The teams exchange lists and are given a time limit in which to work together and decipher the sayings. The team that finishes its list first, or gets the most done within the time limit, wins.

Variations:

1. Titles of books or songs can be used instead of sayings. As with sayings, they should be familiar to all in the group.

2. First lines of poems or songs can also be used, or Scripture passages. A limit should be set on the number of words if first lines of poems or songs, or Scripture verses are used.

Purpose or Benefit

"Hidden Sayings" is a fairly simple word game that can easily be adapted to provide the benefits of teamwork.

Scrambled People

Number of Players:	2-20
Length of Time:	20-60 minutes
Materials:	Paper Pencils
Preparation:	The leader prepares a number of names with the letters scrambled (e.g., YIMJM RTCRAE). These should be written large enough so that all members on a team can read them. On the back of the papers in smaller letters the answers should be written (e.g., Jimmy Carter).
Object of the Game:	To unscramble the names.

To Play:

The group is divided into two teams. The leader shows a scrambled name to the first team. The first person on the team has 30 seconds to unscramble the name and guess. If that person cannot guess, his entire team has 10 seconds to guess. If the name still has not been guessed correctly, the opposing team has five seconds to guess. Five points are given if the first person guesses it correctly; two points if his team guesses it correctly, and three points are awarded to the opposing team if it guesses the name correctly.

The process is repeated for the other team, then alternately for each team until all have had a turn to be the starting player.

Variation:

The two teams go into separate rooms and write scrambled names. They then come out and show the scrambled names to the defending team's first person. Thirty seconds are allowed to guess. If the name is guessed correctly, five points are awarded the defending team. If not guessed, the entire defending team has 10 seconds to guess. If guessed correctly, two points are awarded. If not guessed correctly, the challenging team is awarded three points.

Comments:

Categories could be specified, such as authors, actors, biblical people, historical figures, current event figures, or friends.

Purpose or Benefit

"Scrambled People" demands quick verbal exercise and may also involve teamwork.

Subtitles

Number of Players:	6-20
Length of Time:	20-60 minutes
Materials:	Large pieces of paper Pen/magic markers
Preparation:	The game can be played two ways—either the leader of the game can make up cards with the subtitles and

write them out for the teams to guess, or the teams can make them up for each other to guess. If the leader does not, then his only preparation is to gather the materials.

Object of the Game: To guess the title of a book from a fictitious "subtitle" that has been created for the book.

To Play:

Designate a person to watch the time and keep score. The players are divided into equal teams. If the leader has not prepared the subtitles, the teams go to separate rooms and write on cards a number of fictitious subtitles for titles of books that would be known to all playing. These are the clues from which the other team must try to guess the correct titles.

For example, *Gone with the Wind* could be subtitled "A Breezy Departure," or *Mutiny on the Bounty* could be "The Crew Takes Over," etc.

When the teams return with their subtitles, the leader shows the cards to the teams, alternating between each team. The first person on the guessing team has 15 seconds to guess the correct title; if he does so, the team receives three points. If not, the team can consult together and make another guess; if they succeed together they receive two points. If the cards were made up ahead by the leader, the opposing team can have 10 seconds to consult and make a guess, receiving one point if they are successful.

Comments:

The subtitles should be elusive enough to make guessing difficult, but yet not so vague as to be impossible.

Purpose or Benefit

"Subtitles" is a guessing game that encourages creativity and teamwork.

The Coming of the Sandman

Number of Players: 6-20

Length of Time: 30 minutes

Physical Set-up: A completely darkened room with plenty of walking space

Preparation: Furniture may need to be moved out of the way.

Object of the Game: To guess who the sandman is.

To Play:

One person is the "night watchman." The others decide among themselves which player will be the "sandman," without letting the night watchman know.

The room is darkened to allow the sandman to be invisible. He then touches other players on the head as they wander around. When a player is touched on the head, he falls asleep by dropping silently to the floor.

When another player discovers (or trips over) a sleeping player he says, "Ho-hum," and the sleeper snores audibly. These responses are the night watchman's cue to turn on the light, at which point all the players must freeze. Any other sleepers may also start snoring at this point.

The night watchman now has an opportunity to guess which player is the sandman. If he guesses wrong, he turns out the light so the sandman can continue his work. The sleepers move out of the way before the next round begins.

The game continues as before until the night watchman guesses correctly or is stricken by the sandman himself. (The sandman may tap the night watchman only after all the other players are asleep.) The game can be repeated with a new sandman and a new night watchman.

Comments:

Players should walk carefully to avoid trampling the sleepers.

Removing shoes is advisable.

Purpose or Benefit

"The Coming of the Sandman" is humorous, dramatic, and suspenseful.

Famous Characters

Number of Players:	6-100
Length of Time:	15-45 minutes
Materials:	Name tags Pins or tape
Preparation:	Names of famous people are written on name tags in advance.
Object of the Game:	To find out what name is on your back.

To Play:

The name of a different famous person is fixed on the back of everyone in the group. Each person simultaneously tries to find out the name on his back by asking different people yes-and-no questions about his character. They should ask each person one or two questions. The first person to correctly guess the name on his back wins.

Variations:

1. Each player keeps track of how many questions he asks. Whoever guesses with the least questions wins.

2. It sometimes works best to limit the number of questions people can ask, depending on the amount of time.

Comments:

The famous characters may be past or present, real or fictitious, or even famous animals. However, it is best to use only names that are sure to be known to everyone; it is almost impossible to guess the name of a person one has never heard of or knows very little about.

Purpose or Benefit

"Famous Characters" is a good icebreaker. It can be easily played by a large group as people are arriving.

Going to the Moon

Number of Players:	4-15
Length of Time:	15-30 minutes
Preparation:	At least two players should know the "pattern" of the game before starting. It is also better if the two persons do not sit next to each other.
Object of the Game:	To figure out the pattern that determines what words are acceptable.

To Play:

One of the players who knows the pattern says, "I'm going to the moon and I'm going to take (noun)." The noun fits the pattern, which is unknown to most of the others. The next player then says, "I'm going to the moon and I'm going to take (noun)." That noun is subject to the approval of the two players who know the pattern, and it will be rejected if it does not fit the pattern.

Game then continues around the table with the two knowledgeable players always saying something that fits the pattern and determining if the other players have said something that also fits.

Play progresses until most or all of the others have figured out the pattern.

Suggested patterns:

1. All items must start with the same letter as the person's own first name. Examples: John names anything that starts with "j," Mike names anything that starts with "m," etc.

2. Each item begins with the last letter of the previous item mentioned, whether that item was accepted or not. Example: Do*g* could be followed by *G*lue, which would be followed by *E*lephant.

3. Each item has a "double" letter in it. Examples: b*ee*f, co*o*kie, pi*zz*a, blo*tt*er, baseba*ll*, b*oo*k, pe*nny*, etc.

4. Any other pattern that has enough possibilities that fit it.

Comments:

Guessing the pattern may be frustrating. Encouragement and clues should be given.

Purpose or Benefit

"Going to the Moon" challenges players' deductive reasoning.

Guess the Spice

Number of Players:	4-40
Length of Time:	15-30 minutes
Materials:	Eight or more spices Paper cups Paper Pencils
Preparation:	A sample of each spice is placed in an open, unmarked container, such as a paper cup. Each container is marked with a number. A master list is made of the numbers and their corresponding spices.
Object of the Game:	To identify each spice.

To Play:

Each spice is passed around for each participant to examine by sight and smell *only* (no tasting allowed!). They then write on their papers the numbers of the spice containers and what spice they think each one is. Each spice container may be passed around the circle a maximum of two or three times.

The correct answers are then read from the master list and the players correct their own papers. The winner is the player with the most correct answers.

Variation:

"Guess the Cheese": When cheese is used it should be cut in small cubes and each variety put on a separate, numbered plate. There should be at least as many cubes for each variety as players. Each player may take a cube of each variety and guess by looking, touching, smelling, and tasting.

Purpose or Benefit

"Guess the Spice" challenges the players' knowledge and memory of the spices.

House Detective

Number of Players:	5-25
Length of Time:	30 minutes
Materials:	An assortment of articles normally found in a home Pencils Paper
Playing Site:	Several rooms in a house
Special Requirement:	This is best played with players who are not overly familiar with your home.
Preparation:	The person conducting the game sets objects around his/her home in rooms where they are not normally found (e.g., a can of motor oil on the kitchen counter, a rolling pin in the living room, etc.).
	The leader makes a list of the rooms

being used for each player.

Object of the Game: To guess which items in each room are not normally there.

To Play:

The leader explains the game and distributes the lists to the players. They are given a set time limit to go to each room (15 minutes for four rooms is good).

Within this time the players try to discover and write down the objects that are out of place in each room. When the time is up, they all gather and compare lists.

The person(s) with the most correct items is the winner.

Variation:

Instead of unusual objects placed in the rooms, some things in the rooms are changed. The players are first given an opportunity to go to each room and study it carefully (a time limit for this should be set).

After this the leader goes into each room and makes a change. The participants then go into each room with their lists and record the changes they think have occurred.

This is a good game to play soon after the guests have arrived.

Purpose or Benefit

"House Detective" gets players moving around and is a good icebreaker. The variation challenges observation and memory.

Huckle-Buckle-Beanstalk

Number of Players: 3-15

Length of Time: 10-60 minutes

Materials: Small, identifiable object, such as a thimble, knick-knack, or toy, about 1" to 2" long

Object of the Game: To find the hidden object.

To Play:

After the group is shown the object, one person is appointed to hide it. Everyone else leaves the room. The person places the object somewhere within a room or designated area where others can see it without moving anything to do so. The others may have to look from an unusual angle, but the view must be unobstructed from at least one perspective.

When the object is hidden, the person who hid it says, "Huckle-Buckle-Beanstalk," which signals the others to return. They all look for the hidden object.

If a player spies the object, he leaves it where it is and says, "Huckle-Buckle-Beanstalk" and sits down. It is more considerate to pretend to continue searching for a few moments before saying, "Huckle-Buckle-Beanstalk," and allow the other players to find the object for themselves.

When everyone has found the object, the first person to find it becomes the person who hides it for the next game; or, players may prefer to rotate to insure that everyone gets a turn.

Comments:

Participants may be surprised at how difficult it can be to find something that is in plain sight.

Purpose or Benefit

"Huckle-Buckle-Beanstalk" is good for both children and adults. It encourages inquisitiveness and creativity.

What's in the Bag?

Number of Players: 5-30

Length of Time: 10-30 minutes

Materials: At least 10 paper bags
A kitchen utensil for each bag
Paper and pencil for each player

Preparation:	In advance, 10 or more kitchen utensils are chosen and each one put in a separate, numbered bag.
Object of the Game:	To guess what utensil is in each bag.

To Play:

Players should sit in a circle. Each bag is passed around the circle. After feeling the outside of the bag, each player writes down the number of the bag and his corresponding guess as to what is inside. Each bag may be passed around a maximum of two or three times.

The game is ended by opening each bag and revealing what was inside. The winner is the player with the most correct guesses.

Purpose or Benefit

"What's in the Bag?" can be played equally well by large and small groups.

Wink

Number of Players:	6-15
Length of Time:	20-60 minutes
Materials:	One playing card for each player Candle (optional)
Preparation:	The room may be darkened by dimming the lights or placing a candle in the center as the only illumination.
Object of the Game:	To identify the winker before being winked at.

To Play:

Players are seated in a circle, usually on the floor.

One of the cards is identified as the winker's card. The cards are shuffled and dealt, one to each player. The winker knows who he is, when he receives the winker's card, but does not tell the other players.

The winker tries to catch the other players' eyes and wink at them. Anyone who looks the winker in the eye and is winked at is out.

The person winked at should wait a few moments before he announces he is out so as not to reveal the winker. After he removes himself from the game to be a spectator, the game continues.

The other players try to detect who the winker is before they are "winked out." A player may guess the identity of the winker at any time, but a wrong guess puts him out.

A round ends when the winker is caught, or when only one player remains. The cards are redistributed for the next round.

Variations:

1. Players must maintain eye contact with the other players throughout the game.

2. Having two to four winkers adds excitement in a large group. Winkers try to wink other winkers out, as well, and avoid being winked out themselves.

3. Rather than winking, the winker is a "squeezer" who eliminates other players through a system of hand squeezing. In this variation, all players hold hands in the circle. The squeezer decides who he will "put the squeeze on," then squeezes the person's hand next to him as many times as the "victim" is away from him.

   For example, if the victim is three persons from the squeezer, the squeezer squeezes the adjacent person's hand three times. Then the person whose hand was just squeezed squeezes the next person's hand two times. Then the person whose hand was squeezed twice squeezes the next person's hand *once*. That person announces that he is out and removes himself from the circle.

4. Nonwinkers can guess who the winker is only after two to four people have gone out.

Comments:

The winker must wink distinctly enough so that players do not confuse winks for blinks.

Uniform lighting is essential in larger groups. Many people cannot see a wink if they are sitting next to a light.

Purpose or Benefit

"Wink" produces suspense and excitement. It challenges players to use self-control, caution, and perceptiveness.

MEMORY AND QUICK-THINKING GAMES

These games challenge memory and concentration abilities, and provide exercise in fast thinking in pressure situations. This section includes:

> Memory Games
> Quick-Thinking Circle Games

The combination of skill and entertainment is a beneficial aspect of these games. They are especially enjoyed by older children and adults.

Add-a-Word

Number of Players: 2-20

Length of Time: 10-30 minutes

Object of the Game: To remember all the words given pre-
                      viously.

To Play:

The first player starts a sentence with one word. The next
player repeats the first player's word and adds another word,
and so on. If a player forgets any previous words, that player
leaves the game.

Example:
    First player says: Jesus.
    Second player says: Jesus loves.
    Third player says: Jesus loves you.
    Fourth player says: Jesus loves you now.
    Fifth player says: Jesus loves you and . . . (forgetting now).

The fifth player leaves the game and the next player starts another sentence.

The last remaining player wins.

Variation:

Each player adds a sentence or a phrase, the purpose being to
make an interesting story. Everyone remains in the game.
Word-for-word accuracy is not essential.

Purpose or Benefit

"Add-a-Word" provides quiet, creative, sometimes humorous,
entertainment, and requires concentration. This game is especially good for children.

Alphabetical Shopping List

Number of Players: 5-30

Length of Time: 15-30 minutes

Object of the Game: To remember all the items named.

To Play:

Players take turns saying: "I went to the store and bought
_____." The first person fills in the blank with an item begin-
ning with the letter "A" (e.g., "apples").

Each successive person repeats the sentence as the previous
one said it, and then adds the phrase: "and _____," filling in
the blank with an item beginning with the next letter of the alphabet. For example, the second person might add "ba-
nanas."

When a player forgets an item previously named, he is out of
the game.

If more than one player is able to remember the items for the
entire alphabet, the game can be continued by adding adjectives beginning with the same letters as the items (e.g., "appealing apple," "beautiful boat," etc.). The game ends when
only one player is left, who becomes the winner.

Variation:

Each player says, "I'm going on a trip and I'm taking a
_____."

Purpose or Benefit

"Alphabetical Shopping List" can easily be played to help
pass a waiting period.

Eyewitness

Number of Players: 4-30

Length of Time: 30-90 minutes

Materials:	Paper
	Pencils
	Costume clothing (optional)

Playing Site: A separate room should be available for consultation and costuming.

Preparation: Clothing is gathered which could be used as costumes if it is decided to use them.

Object of the Game: To observe and remember with the greatest accuracy the actions that are performed.

To Play:

One or two people chosen to perform for the group go into separate rooms to plan their performance. They may also put on costumes.

Pencils and paper are passed out to the rest of the players.

After 5-10 minutes, the actors return and perform a skit or a series of actions in mime (i.e., without speaking).

When the performers are finished, the players write down for about 5 minutes as many of the actions that they have just witnessed as they can remember.

Each person reads aloud what he has written. The one who has remembered the most actions the most accurately is judged the winner by the actor(s).

Variation:

"Eyewitness" can be played by breaking down into small groups. After seeing the performance, the small groups have separate consultations to pool their memories.

Comments:

Breaking down into small groups may be preferable when there is a large number of players.

It may be helpful to have the actors write down a list of the actions they are going to use: That way they will be clear on what actions to perform and will be better able to judge who has remembered the best.

Purpose or Benefit

"Eyewitness" increases players' ability to observe and remember. It is a challenge to play by small groups, because each group of people must come to agreement about what they saw.

Group Concentration

Number of Players:	9-25
Length of Time:	30-90 minutes
Materials:	Paper Pencils
Playing Site:	Best played in a building (house) with several rooms
Object of the Game:	To remember and recite the story correctly.

To Play:

The players are split into groups of four to seven people each. The groups then separate into isolated rooms to prepare their stories. Each group jointly writes one story. The stories should be four to five sentences long with lots of details. The sentences do not necessarily need to flow smoothly when read.

An example would be: "Mr. Jones, the head supervisor at the IGA store on the corner of Albert and Steel Roads, caught an elementary-aged schoolboy shoplifting in his store. It was a hot, muggy, spring afternoon when a red-headed man walked to the bank to get some extra change. The stoplight was broken and the policeman blew his tin whistle at all of the pedestrians who were trying to get to Roosevelt Park to see the Little League baseball team's victory parade. Mrs. Anderson felt faint as she sat in her new bentwood rocker on the porch, knitting the green and yellow baby blanket for her great niece's new baby girl, Carmen."

The purpose behind making the story incomplete or nonsensical is to hinder the person hearing the story from remembering what he has been told. This is accomplished by using many details and making the story line "choppy." When each group has completed its story, the groups meet together in a common room.

One player from each group is chosen to be their group's reader. Then, one group (group #1) is asked to leave the room and wait in an adjacent room where they cannot hear what is said in the common room. One person from the group remains. All other groups remain seated. The reader from one of the remaining groups then reads his group's story to person #1. The story cannot be read more than two times. Next, one more person from group #1 re-enters the room (person #2). Person #1 repeats the story to person #2, not more than one time. Another person (person #3) is then asked in from group #1 and person #2 repeats the story to him—only once. This continues until the last person from group #1 has heard and repeated the story. The original story is then read again for the benefit of group #1, and to compare it with the last version related.

Once group #1 has finished, a new group leaves the common room with the exception of one person. The reader from group #1 then reads his group's story to this person and the game continues, using the same procedure used with group #1. The game is finished when each group has had a chance to read its story and to listen to a story from another group.

Variation:

The stories can be prepared in advance and simply handed out to each group, thus saving time.

Comments:

The more people playing, the larger the groups should be, and the more fun it will be to play.

Children under nine years old may have a hard time playing this game.

Purpose or Benefit

"Group Concentration" is a good exercise in careful listening and inevitably produces humorous "miscommunications."

Memory Game

Number of Players:	6-25
Length of Time:	10-15 minutes
Materials:	A large serving tray
	At least 20 small items—e.g., bobby pins, spool of thread, safety pin, tack, spoon, box of matches, etc. (The more items, the better.) Paper, pencil and writing surface for each player
Preparation:	The tray is filled with the small items. They are arranged so that each one is in plain sight. The tray is then hidden or covered until the game is played.
Object of the Game:	To list all the items on the tray.

To Play:

Each player is given a paper, pencil, and writing surface. The leader carries the uncovered tray around to each of the players, allowing each player a few seconds to look.

After each player has seen the tray, it is removed or covered. The players then list as many items as they can remember from looking at the tray.

When the players have finished writing, the tray is returned. Players may check their own papers or exchange with one another. The game leader names each item on the tray. The player with the greatest number of items correctly named is the winner.

Purpose or Benefit

This game is a good test of memory and easy for people to play who are unfamiliar with each other.

Ali Baba and the Forty Thieves

Number of Players: 6-12

Length of Time: 15-45 minutes

Object of the Game: To achieve a continuously changing set of actions around a circle.

To Play:

One person is chosen to be the leader. This player must perform some motion (e.g., clapping hands) to the rhythm of the words, "Al-i-Ba-ba and the Forty Thieves." As soon as he completes the rhyme once, the player to his right repeats the motion and player #1 must simultaneously perform a *different* motion (e.g., patting his head) to the same rhythm. Thereafter, the leader must start a new motion each time the rhyme is repeated, with each player repeating whatever the player on his left has just completed. Play continues around the circle until everyone is doing a different motion and repeating the rhyme, or until one of the players gets confused and is unable to keep the motion going. At this point, a new leader is chosen.

Variations:

1. Alternating going clockwise and counterclockwise around the circle will add variety.

2. Another rhythm such as a Bible verse, a line to a song, etc., may be used.

Comments:

"Ali Baba and the Forty Thieves" is more difficult than meets the eye, but players improve with practice. Older children will enjoy this game, as well as adults. It can easily be played outside as well.

Purpose or Benefit

"Ali Baba and the Forty Thieves" promotes group participation and teamwork, and also requires some concentration. The leader is challenged to think quickly and creatively, and can adjust the difficulty of the game to the ability of the particular group.

Alphabet Game

Number of Players: 2-10

Length of Time: 10-30 minutes

Object: of the Game: To think of as many words as possible for each letter of the alphabet, for a certain topic.

To Play:

A topic is chosen, such as Christmas, names of cities, cars, animals, etc. Each person in the group then takes a turn, going around the circle, thinking of and saying a word beginning with A. After everyone has had a turn, they start with the letter B, and so on through the alphabet. A player is "out" if he cannot think of an appropriate word on his turn.

Variation:

Players may progress through the alphabet consecutively. For example, player 1 must think of a word starting with A, player 2 must think of a word starting with B, player 3 one starting with C, and so on through the alphabet. A player is "out" if he cannot think of a word starting with the correct letter on his turn. The game can go through the alphabet as many times as the players choose.

Comments:

Players may wish to set a time limit on how long a player can think on his turn.

Purpose or Benefit

The "Alphabet Game" provides an opportunity for thinking and informal interacting.

The Animal Game

Number of Players: 5-20

Length of Time: 30-60 minutes

Materials: One or two decks of Rook ® cards

Object of the Game: To accumulate the most cards.

To Play:

Each player identifies himself as an animal with a corresponding animal call. For example, a dog has a call of "bow-wow." No two players may choose the same animal call.

The cards are dealt so that each player has the same number of cards, or as nearly so as possible. *Two decks may be used for larger groups.*

Each player places his cards in a stack, face down in front of him. The player to the dealer's left turns over his top card so that all may see it. The second player to the left does the same and so on around the table, until a player turns over a card that is the same number as a previous player's exposed card—for example, a Green 3 and a Black 3.

The two players with the equal number cards each try to be the first to recite the other's animal call. Thus, if a pig has a Green 3 and a dog has a Black 3, dog tries to say "oink-oink" before pig can say "bow-wow."

The player who finishes the other's call first is awarded the other players' stack of face-up cards.

Play then resumes at the point it left off. Each player keeps his face-up cards stacked so that only the last one played is exposed. The game continues until one player has all the cards or until a time or endurance limit is met.

Comments:

"The Animal Game" becomes more challenging and more amusing with a larger group.

Purpose or Benefit

"The Animal Game" is humorous, even hilarious, and requires alertness and a keen memory.

Buzz

Number of Players: 6

Length of Time: 15-45 minutes

Object of the Game: To say "buzz" at the appropriate
                      times.

To Play:

Each player takes a seat in a circle. The players count off
around the circle. When a player's turn falls on a multiple of
five, he says "buzz," instead of the number. When a player
fails to do so, he is out. The last player remaining wins.

Variation:

Multiples of any other number may be used instead of five.

Multiples of two numbers are used, with players saying
"buzz" for either.

Comments:

Multiples of five are good for younger children.

Purpose or Benefit

"Buzz" is a fun way for children to learn multiples. It encourages alertness and self-control. The variations make it a challenging game for adults.

Earth, Air, Water

Number of Players: 2-20

Length of Time: 15-60 minutes

Materials: Ball, balloon, or similar object

Object of the Game: To name some creature that dwells in
                      the environment given (earth, air, or
                      water) before the balloon comes down
                      or the object being rolled reaches the
                      player.

To Play:

The players are seated around a table, or in a circle around a room. The first player pronounces the category of "earth," "air," or "water," just before he either tosses a balloon in the air or rolls a ball or some other object to another player. As he sets the balloon or ball in motion, he calls out the other player's name.

Before the balloon lands or the ball reaches him, the other player must name a creature that dwells in the category he is given by the first player.

He then tosses the balloon or rolls the ball to another player, calling out a category and the player's name. A player may not name a creature (animal, bird, insect, fish, reptile, etc.) that has been previously mentioned.

If a player names a creature that has been previously used, or cannot think of one before the object reaches him, he is out of the game. The game is played until all are out except the winner.

Variations:

1. To make the game easier, instead of naming living creatures such as kinds of birds, animals, fish, etc., anything that exists on the earth, flies through the air, or goes through water can be named (e.g., "airplane" or "rocket" would be suitable answers for "air," or "boat" or "submarine" for water, etc.).

2. Instead of going out, players can take a letter of the word "OUT." The first time they cannot name a creature, they get an "O," and so on, until they have spelled the word "OUT."

Purpose or Benefit

"Earth, Air, Water" challenges players' knowledge of kinds of animals, birds, fish, etc., and their ability to think quickly.

Famous People

Number of Players: 2-20

Length of Time: 5-30 minutes

Object of the Game: To name a new famous person on cue.

To Play:

The first player begins by saying the first and last name of a famous person. The next player must name a person whose first name begins with the first letter of the previously mentioned person's *last* name.

For example, if the first person says, "George Washington," the next player could say, "Winston Churchill," and the next player, "Christopher Columbus," and so on.

When a player is unable to think of a new person beginning with the letter he is given, within a specified time limit, he is "out." The last person to go out is the winner.

Variation:

To make the game more difficult, the famous people that can be mentioned can be limited to certain categories, such as "living," "dead," "authors," "Americans," "Biblical characters," etc.

Purpose or Benefit

"Famous People" is lighthearted, requires little instruction, and can be played anywhere for any length of time. It makes a good travel game.

The Fruit Game

Number of Players: 5-15

Length of Time: 25-45 minutes

Material: Rolled-up newspaper or other harmless "club"

Object of the Game: To keep from being "it" (the person standing in the middle). For "it" to gain a place in the circle.

To Play:

Each player chooses the name of a fruit to be his for the game. No two players may have the same name.

The group sits in a circle. One player stands in the center, holding the rolled-up newspaper.

A player begins the game by saying the name of his fruit followed by the name of another player's fruit. The person whose fruit name the first player adds to his own must then repeat his own name and add another's name.

Sample game sequence: Apple says, "Apple-raspberry," then Raspberry says, "Raspberry-grape," then Grape says, "Grape-pear," etc.

Using the newspaper, the person who is "it" tries to strike the head of the player whose fruit name has just been called before that player finishes saying his and another's fruit name. He continues to try as the players continue their fruit name sequence.

When "it" succeeds, he takes the seat of the player he has intercepted; the player he has intercepted becomes "it," and the game continues.

Variations:

1. The word "loves" may be inserted between the fruit names (e.g., "apple loves pear").

2. Instead of fruit, names of famous people, minor prophets, disciples, fruit of the Spirit, months of the year, animal names, etc., may be used.

3. Each person selects a gesture to portray a given animal. One person starts the game by performing his gesture and then the gesture of another person. That person then performs his gesture and someone else's. Play continues as above.

4. Rather than using a newspaper, a pair of cotton socks (one inside the other) may be used.

Comments:

The person who is "it" should take care not to get carried away in striking the other players.

Purpose or Benefit

"The Fruit Game" is suspenseful and calls for quick thinking. It is a good icebreaker; it helps people to loosen up. The game is especially good for high school and college students.

Geography

Number of Players: 2-12

Length of Time: 10-30 minutes

Object of the Game: To always think of a new place when it is your turn.

To Play:

Someone begins by saying the name of a place (country, city, state, etc.). The next person must say the name of a place that starts with the last letter of the place the first person named, and so on around the group. A typical sequence might be: Missouri—Ionia—America.

No one may use the name of a place already mentioned. If someone cannot think of a place with the right letter on his turn, he is out of the game. The last player remaining wins.

Variations:

1. To make the game more difficult, the geography can be limited in a certain way. For example, only cities can be named, or only places out of the United States can be named, etc.

2. Instead of naming a place that begins with the last letter of the previously mentioned place, the players just go through the alphabet and each must name a place beginning with the letter that falls on his turn.

3. A certain word is chosen with a variety of letters, such as

"geography" or "Argentina." Each player in turn must name a place beginning with each successive letter of the word. This works best if the number of letters in the word chosen is not equal to, or a multiple of, the number of people in the room so that everyone gets a different letter each time.

Purpose or Benefit

This is a challenging game that is fun, and also serves as a refresher in geography.

The Minister's Cat

Number of Players: 5-15

Length of Time: 30-60 minutes

Object of the Game: To think of as many adjectives as possible, beginning with each letter of the alphabet.

To Play:

All the players sit in a circle.

The phrase used throughout the game is: "The minister's cat is a _____ cat." Beginning with the letter A, and going around the circle, each person fills in an adjective to describe the cat.

When someone cannot think of an adjective beginning with A, he misses and the next person begins with B. The game continues through the letter Z.

If any of the players uses an adjective that has already been used, that is considered a miss, and the next person goes on to the next letter.

Purpose or Benefit

"The Minister's Cat" is a traditional, lighthearted game which helps people to think creatively.

One, Two, Three, You're an Elephant

Number of Players: 7-20

Length of Time: 15-30 minutes

Object of the Game: To avoid being "it."

To Play:

The players sit in a circle. One of the players is chosen to be "it" and stands in the center of the circle.

The player in the center, trying to surprise individuals in the circle, points to them and says, "1, 2, 3, you're an elephant!" The player he points to and the players on either side must respond before he finishes the sentence.

The player pointed to must make his hands into fists and put them in front of his nose to form a "trunk," and the players on each side must put their cupped hands up to his ears to form "ears." Any of the three who is too slow replaces the person in the center and the game continues.

Comments:

Speed is the essential ingredient in this game. The player chosen to be "it" must be quick if he is to catch the other players off guard. The players sitting in a circle must also be quick if they are to avoid being caught off guard.

Purpose or Benefit

This game takes quick reflexes, coordination and a sense of humor. "1, 2, 3, You're an Elephant" is also a great icebreaker.

Rhythm Game

Number of Players: 6-30

Length of Time: 15-60 minutes

Object of the Game: To get to the #1 seat in the circle.

To Play:

Players sit in a circle and number off starting with #1, to the last player.

Throughout the actual play of the game, the players keep a rhythm going with their hands, keeping in time with each other. Each player slaps his lap twice, claps his hands twice, snaps his left fingers once, and snaps his right fingers once, with an equal amount of time between each of the six beats: slap-slap-clap-clap-snap-snap.

Once the rhythm is going, player #1 begins by saying his number as he snaps his left fingers and saying another player's number as he snaps his right fingers.

The player whose number he called must then, in the next rhythm sequence, say his own number as he snaps his left fingers, and another player's number as he snaps his right fingers.

The turn to speak is volleyed about the circle in this way until a player fails to say the appropriate numbers, in rhythm, on the next snaps that occur after his number is called.

When a player misses, he must take the seat in the circle of the last player (the highest number). All those who were after him move up one seat and are assigned a new number (one number less than their previous one).

The rhythm is resumed, and #1 begins the volley again. Play may continue indefinitely.

Variations:

1. Rhymes: Instead of being assigned numbers, the players are assigned words that rhyme with the first one. Thus, a typical sequence would be: "cat-fat," "fat-sat," "sat-gnat."

2. Names: The player speaking must say his name and another player's name on each snap.

Comments:

For children who cannot snap their fingers or remember so many movements, the rhythm can be alternated to be "slap-slap-slap-slap-clap-clap," with the numbers, rhymes or names called out on the claps.

Purpose or Benefit

"Rhythm" helps players to develop a sense of rhythm and to think fast.

The name variation is an effective way to get to know people's names.

The Sign Game

Number of Players: 6-12

Length of Time: 15-45 minutes

Object of the Game: To give the proper signs on turn.

To Play:

Each player chooses a "sign" with which to identify himself. Examples: scratching his nose, snapping his fingers, slapping his stomach. Any nonverbal expression that everyone can do is permissible.

Someone begins the game by performing his sign, following it with another person's sign. The person whose sign he performed must respond by giving his sign, and then someone else's.

If a player fails to respond immediately or if he gives the sign of someone who is no longer in the game, he is eliminated from the game. Play continues until there is only one person remaining, who then wins.

Everyone not actually performing a sign slaps his knees with both hands, to keep a rhythm going and add to the suspense. This also allows players to participate after they are excluded from play.

Variations:

1. Each person chooses a different *animal* to pretend to be, and decides upon a gesture which would characterize that animal. For example, an appropriate gesture with which to characterize an elephant would be leaning over with arms

straight and hands clasped. The game proceeds as above.

2. Players cannot respond *back* to the person who gestured to them. For example, if player A gestures to player B, player B cannot do his own gesture and then player A's again.

3. A metronome may be used to create a tempo (rather than players slapping their knees). In this case, the tempo may be speeded up as the game progresses.

Comments:

Creativity and diversity among signs will make the game more humorous.

Purpose or Benefit

"The Sign Game" challenges the memories and the actions of participants. It is also humorous, and loosens inhibitions.

Telegraph

Number of Players:	5-20
Length of Time:	10-30 minutes
Object of the Game:	To pass "squeezes" around the circle without being caught by the person in the center.

To Play:

The players sit or stand in a circle, holding hands. One person is out of the room and the other players agree on who will start the squeeze. The person comes back into the room and stands in the center of the circle.

The player starts by squeezing the hand of the person to the left or right of him. That player can then either squeeze back or send it to the next player, and so on.

The player in the center tries to catch someone who has received the squeeze before he can pass it on. He says, "You!" or "There!" pointing to the person.

If a player is caught, he goes out of the room and the group decides again who will start the squeeze, and the game continues.

Comments:

Players should not try to hide or disguise their squeezes. Hands must be in plain view.

"Telegraph" will probably be frustrating for children younger than junior high age.

Purpose or Benefit

There is much working together in this game. Concentration is required and suspense is generated.

WORD, THINKING, AND QUIET GAMES

Many of these games are traditionally popular games. They include:

Word Games
Paper-and-Pencil Thinking Games
Quiet Circle Games

The word games are long-standing favorites with some creative variations. The paper-and-pencil games can be enjoyed by older children and adults. Quiet circle games are traditional children's games which adults may want to engage in for a change of pace.

Anagrab

Number of Players:	2-8
Length of Time:	40-60 minutes
Materials:	Letter tiles from a Scrabble ® game Good dictionary
Playing Site:	Players are seated around a table
Object of the Game:	To possess as many words as possible at the end of the game.

To Play:

The letter tiles are face down in the center of the table.

The first player exposes a tile, leaving it in the center of the table. The person on his left does likewise, and so on around the table. As soon as four tiles have been exposed, any player may call out a word, following these rules:

1. The word must be four or more letters long.

2. The word must be legitimate by the standards the group sets at the beginning of the game. For example, proper nouns may be excluded. Words pluralized by "s" are unacceptable.

3. Each word must include one or more letters from the pool of exposed letters in the middle.

4. A player may use the letters of any word already formed by someone, combining them with letters from the pool. He must use all the letters from the old word, however.

5. Only exposed letters from the pool and words already formed may be used to create new words.

6. If a word taken from another player is used, the letters must be rearranged so that the same root word is not used again.

The letters of each word called are placed in front of the caller, facing the other players. When a caller uses the letters from someone else's word to form his word, he captures the tiles of that word and arranges them as the new word at his place.

If a new tile is exposed that no player can use, it is left in the pool, face-up, and another tile is exposed. If there are several tiles in the pool, players use as many of these as possible before adding any more to the pool.

In case of a tie in calling a word, the letters go to the player whose word has the most letters. If the two tie words are of the same length, no one takes the letters, and neither word may be used for the rest of the game.

A new word may be challenged by anyone at the table at the time it is called. A dictionary may be used to settle any disputes. If the word is unacceptable, the player who called it may not call again until after two more tiles have been exposed.

The game ends when either the pool is empty and there are no more new letters to add to it, or when all the players agree that no more new words can be formed using the remaining letters in the pool.

Scores are determined as follows: For each word, the point values indicated on each tile are added together. This sum is multiplied by the number of letters in the word. Then the total points thus determined for each word are added together to indicate the player's final score. The player with the highest score wins.

Comments:

"Anagrab" is particularly appealing to those who enjoy quick-thinking games requiring verbal ability.

"Anagrab" requires considerable concentration as well as speed. Therefore, the strategy of waiting for a particular letter to be exposed is not recommended.

Purpose or Benefit

Players are challenged to think quickly and to exercise concentration and vocabulary skills.

Conglomeration

Number of Players:	2-20
Length of Time:	15-45 minutes
Materials:	Paper and pencil for each player Dictionary
Object of the Game:	To form as many words as possible which are different from those formed by other players.

To Play:

A long word such as "conglomeration" is selected by the leader as the source word. This word is announced to the players, and the correct spelling is given. The players write it on the tops of their papers.

A time limit is set by the leader. During this time the players try to form as many words as possible using only the letters in the source word. Each letter can be used only as many times as it appears in the source word. Usually proper names and plurals are not allowed.

At the end of the time limit, each player reads his words. Each player gets a point for any word he has that *no one else has.* The player with the most points wins.

If there is some doubt as to whether a word exists that a player has formed, the dictionary is consulted by the leader.

Variations:

1. The game can be played using proper names of persons or places as source words. For example, "Baltimore, Maryland," or "Boston, Massachusetts," can be the source. From the letters in the city-state combination, players form the names of as many cities or states in the United States as possible. A long proper name can be the source (e.g., "Oliver Wendell Holmes)," and from that name the names of as many American authors or poets (or whatever category is chosen) are formed.

2. The game can be played by teams instead of individuals competing against each other. Each team can consult together (three to four persons per team is a good amount) to

form as many words/names as possible from the source word.

Purpose or Benefit

"Conglomeration" challenges one's vocabulary or familiarity with persons or places. When played by teams it promotes co-operation.

Every Other

Number of Players:	2-20
Length of Time:	15-60 minutes
Materials:	Large card or pieces of paper Magic marker Pencils and paper Watch with second hand
Preparation:	The person conducting the game can prepare ahead by writing words on large cards or pieces of paper. When the words are written, however, every other letter, starting with the first, is omitted. For example, the word "waterfall" would be written "_ A _ E _ F _ L _." On a card beside each word a corresponding clue or catchy definition is written. The card for "waterfall" might be written as follows: "_ A _ E _ F _ L _" Clue: "It comes down."
Object of the Game:	To guess correctly as many words as possible, as quickly as possible.

To Play:

The person who prepared the words and clues is the moderator. Anyone who helped prepare the words and clues should not be included among the players.

The players are divided into two equal teams. A captain is chosen for each team. When the moderator holds up a card, one person has 20 seconds to guess the word (without assistance from another player). If this person guesses the word within the allotted time, five points are awarded to his team. He may only guess once during this time. If he does not guess the word correctly, his team has 15 seconds to consult and guess again. This guess must be submitted by the team's captain. If they guess correctly, they are given three points.

If they are incorrect, the opposing team has 10 seconds to consult and try to correctly guess the word. If their guess is successful, they are given two points. If they are unsuccessful, no points are awarded and another word is selected. The teams take turns initiating the guessing, beginning with a different player each time.

The team with the most points after the last word is played is the winner.

Variations:

1. To play "Every Other" with less preparation ahead of time, each team makes up words and clues for the other team. The scoring is the same, except that the team submitting the word and clue are not given the chance to guess. The team submitting the word is awarded five points if the opposing team does not guess correctly.

2. Names of famous people may be used as subject words.

Purpose or Benefit

"Every Other" challenges players' word-sense, and can make them learn to function quickly as a team.

Ghost

Number of Players:	4-10
Length of Time:	20-60 minutes
Material:	Dictionary

Object of the Game: To avoid completing words.

To Play:

The first player names a letter of the alphabet. Each player in turn adds a letter. Each letter added must make the sequence of letters retain the potential for becoming a word. However, no player seeks to actually complete a word, because if he does, he takes a letter from the word "Ghost." Words under four letters in length are not counted as completed words, however.

When a player has spelled the word "Ghost," he is out of the game.

If a player thinks that a letter just named could not allow the letter-chain to become a word, he may challenge the player who named it. The player challenged must then name a word that could eventually be completed by the sequence. If he fails to name a word that can be confirmed by other players or a dictionary, he takes a letter. If he can name one, the challenger takes a letter. When a player cannot add to a word successfully, the next player begins a new word.

The last player to spell the word "Ghost" is the winner.

Variations:

1. A bit trickier version: letters can be added before *or* after the sequence already named to form a word.

2. A very difficult version: letters can be added *between* two letters already named to form a word.

3. *Two* letters are begun with, and added each time, at the beginning or end of the letters already used.

4. For a shorter game the word "Out" is spelled.

Purpose or Benefit

For adults, "Ghost" can be intellectually stimulating. Children can also play, and practice spelling words familiar to them.

Group Password

Number of Players:	6-20
Length of Time:	15-60 minutes
Materials:	2 pencils Small pieces of paper
Object of the Game:	To guess the password in the fewest attempts possible.

To Play:

The players are divided evenly into equal teams. Each team goes to separate rooms to confer. They write a different "password" on each paper for the other team to guess (enough passwords for each member of the opposite team).

After the passwords have been written, the teams come together. Team #1 gives its passwords to team #2, and vice versa.

One player from team #1 draws a password and gives a synonym for it. Each person in team #1 has an opportunity to guess the password. Each guess counts as one point.

The clue-giver may give another clue at any time, but each time he does, his team receives two points. Team #1 continues until the password is guessed.

The process is repeated with team #2. The teams take turns guessing passwords until all the words have been used, with a different clue-giver each time. The group with the lowest total score wins.

Variation:

For a larger group the players are divided into more than two teams. When a player draws a password, he draws one from any of the other teams.

Purpose or Benefit

"Group Password" is a challenge to effective communication.

Jotto

Number of Players:	2
Length of Time:	10-60 minutes
Materials:	2 pencils
	2 pieces of paper
Object of the Game:	To guess the other player's word.

To Play:

Each player selects a word of predetermined length. In an effort to guess the other player's word, one player proposes a word of the given length to his opponent. The other player replies by indicating the number of letters that are common between his secret word and the word which was spoken.

Through interpretation of these responses, each player attempts to discern the word which the other has chosen. The first one to do so wins.

Variation:

It is possible for three to six people to play Jotto together. When this is done, each person proposing a word receives replies from all the other players. The game ends when all the words have been guessed. A player guesses by showing the other players individually, and in writing, what he guesses their respective words to be. If he is incorrect on any of his guesses, he is eliminated from the game except to reply to the other players with regard to *his own* word. The first person to guess all the words wins.

Comments:

When showing written guesses to the other players, it is important to show only one guess to each individual. This safeguards the possibility of divulging information about one of the other player's words.

Purpose or Benefit

"Jotto" requires deductive reasoning and organization of information.

New Password

Number of Players: 6-14

Length of Time: 30-90 minutes

Materials: Paper
    Pencils

Object of the Game: To guess the opposing team's main word.

To Play:

Players divide into two teams. The teams then isolate them-selves into separate rooms to prepare for the game.

First, each team chooses a "main word" (e.g., horse). Then, five "passwords" are chosen. Passwords are words which in some way relate to the main word (e.g., cowboy, ride, reins, donkey, stirrups). Finally, five one-word "clues" are chosen. The clues must relate to the passwords (e.g., hat, sit, bridle, mule, boots). The teams each write their main word, pass-words, and clues on paper and then come together in a com-mon room to play.

One team is chosen to be the guessing team, team B, and the other team becomes team A. Team A gives one clue to the first person on the guessing team (e.g., team A says "hat" to per-son #1). Person #1 then has one guess in which to name the password which the clue relates to (in this case, "cowboy"). If person #1 guesses correctly, he may then guess once at what the main word is ("horse").

If, however, person #1 guessed incorrectly when guessing the password, then team A gives a new clue ("sit") to the second person (person #2) of the guessing team. Person #2 has one guess in which to name the password to which his clue relates (in our example, "ride"). As in the case of person #1, if per-son #2 guesses correctly, he may then have one chance to guess the main word ("horse").

The game continues with team A giving clues one-by-one un-til a player on the guessing team is able to guess the main word. If all five clues are given without team B correctly guessing the main word, team A may begin again by giving five new clues for the five passwords.

When the main word of team A has been guessed, the teams switch roles. Team A then becomes the guessing team and team B gives its clues.

Comments:

The teams may decide on several sets of main words and passwords to give to each other. The team that guesses its main words with the least password exchanges wins.

Teammates should take care to remain quiet during the clue-password exchanges so as not to assist the person guessing.

Purpose or Benefit

"New Password" sharpens one's thinking. It also presents an opportunity for good group planning.

Scrambled Word Game

Number of Players:	5-30
Length of Time:	20-40 minutes
Materials:	Prepared lists Pencils
Preparation:	A list of words suited to an occasion, or based on a theme, are prepared in advance. The spelling of each word is changed by scrambling the letters in it, with no letters being added or removed. The list is copied for distribution.
Object of the Game:	To unscramble as many words as possible in the allotted time.

To Play:

Each player is given a list and a pencil. Players are instructed to discover the original words, by rearranging the letters of the scrambled words listed and writing the correct word beside each scrambled one.

Players are informed of the time limit and warned when the time is almost over. The player with the most correct words wins.

Purpose or Benefit

"Scrambled Word Game" helps develop a theme, and challenges players' verbal and problem-solving skills.

Square Words

Number of Players:	2-20
Length of Time:	20-60 minutes
Materials:	Pencil Paper
Object of the Game:	To form as many words as possible.

To Play:

Each player draws a closed grid with 6 lines, vertically and horizontally, making a square with 25 boxes (see examples). The players take turns calling out letters to place in the square. Each player can place his letters wherever he chooses in his grid. There should be a time limit within which each letter must be chosen, otherwise, there can be long waits for people to decide.

Examples:

t	r	i	t	e
r	e	l	a	x
e	t	n	n	l
c	a	s	k	s
p	m	a	s	h

s	m	e	l	t
t	e	n	t	s
a	s	s	a	r
c	h	a	r	e
k	i	l	e	p

Each player must write his letter in a square before the next letter is called. After all the squares have been filled in, each player figures his score by finding the words he has formed by his placement of the letters. The words can be formed vertically (top to bottom) or horizontally (left to right). 2-letter words = 2 points, 3-letter words = 3 points, etc. The points are totalled and the player with the highest score wins.

Variation:

Backward and diagonal formation can be added if desired.

Purpose or Benefit

"Square Words" exercises language skills, and gives all players a chance to contribute to the challenge created for the other players.

Topical Password

Number of Players:	5
Length of Time:	20-90 minutes
Materials:	Pencils and paper Clock with a second hand
Preparation:	The person who will moderate the game selects at least eight topics and a corresponding sub-topic for each. For instance, if "music" is chosen as a topic, Broadway musicals may be chosen as its sub-topic. The moderator then makes a list of 10 examples for each sub-topic. For instance, examples of Broadway musicals might be "My Fair Lady," "Fiddler on the Roof," etc.
Object of the Game:	To guess as many examples as possible from each category within one minute.

To Play:

Four people divide into pairs. One other person acts as the moderator. The game begins when the moderator announces any four of his topics to the players. At this point each pair decides which person will give clues and which will attempt to guess the correct response.

The moderator then asks one of the pairs which topic they would like to try. Once the choice is made, the moderator gives the list of ten examples for that topic to the person who will be giving the clues. The moderator then informs everyone what the sub-topic is.

As soon as the sub-topic is announced, a 60-second time period begins within which all clues and responses must be given. The person who has the list of examples gives one-word clues to his partner, while his partner tries to guess the examples indicated by his clues. He may give as many clues as he wishes for each example, and may change to another example at any point.

If a clue is given which is part of the example itself, the team cannot receive credit for that example (i.e., "Pacific" would be inappropriate as a clue for "South Pacific").

When 60 seconds have expired, the other pair chooses a topic from the remaining three. The pairs alternate in selecting the final two topics. The clue-giver and responding player for each pair exchange roles to guess the last two topics.

If more topics have been prepared, four more are announced by the moderator and the pair that was the first to choose from the original four now chooses second.

This process continues until no more topics remain. At this point, the number of correct responses are compiled for each pair. The couple with the most correct responses wins.

Variation:

Three or four pairs may play. This does not change the procedure of the game, except that more topics are announced at once. As many topics should be used as there are people playing.

Purpose or Benefit

"Topical Password" challenges one's ability to think quickly and creatively.

Word Bridges

Number of Players:	2-20
Length of Time:	30-45 minutes
Materials:	Paper Pencils
Preparation:	A sheet of paper for each team with the word "bridge" printed on it should be prepared in advance.
Object of the Game:	To produce the longest words possible.

To Play:

Players are divided into equal teams.

Each team is given a piece of paper with a word written on it vertically, then written backwards vertically opposite it, with lines connecting the first and last letters.

EXAMPLES:

```
P_____R       G_____S
L_____E       A_____E
A_____Y  or   M_____M
Y_____A       E_____A
E_____L       S_____G
R_____P
```

After the instructions are given, each team goes to separate rooms, or parts of the room, and has 15 minutes to consult and come up with the longest words possible given their beginning and ending letters (all teams should have the same ones to work with).

The leader of the game should give a warning at 10 minutes that only 5 minutes are left, and another when there is just one minute remaining. (Fifteen minutes is a good time limit for six- to seven-letter words, longer or shorter time limits can be given for longer or shorter words.)

The teams return after 15 minutes and take turns reading their words for each letter. They are awarded one point for each letter of each word. If a word is not in the dictionary, no points are given for it. If a word is misspelled, points are given only for the correct letters.

Purpose or Benefit

"Word Bridges" is a challenging game that encourages team-work and can improve or test vocabulary.

Paper and Pencil Thinking Games

B and T

Number of Players:	3-30
Length of Time:	10-25 minutes
Materials:	Paper for each player
	Pencil for each player
Object of the Game:	To write down the most objects.

To Play:

Each player is given paper and pencil. The players are given three minutes to write down as many objects in the room as they can that start with B or T. The player with the longest list wins.

Variation:

The game can be repeated with other letters.

Comments:

The players should not know what the letters are until just before they begin.

Purpose or Benefit

"B and T" is relaxing, yet challenging.

Categories

Number of Players:	5-15
Length of Time:	20 minutes-2 hours
Materials:	Paper Pencil Writing surface for each player A watch or timer
Preparation:	Papers are prepared having six squares across and six squares down (see example on page 242).
Object of the Game:	To fill in the greatest number of blanks with answers different from other players.

To Play:

Each player is given a paper with squares marked off. As a group, the players decide on five categories to be written across the top (e.g., sports, nations, famous people), one for each of five squares (see example).

The categories should be made clear (e.g., famous people use last name, living or dead, real or imaginary). The group then picks a five-letter word with no letters repeated (e.g., "paper" with two p's would not be used). The letters of the word are placed in the squares on the left side (see example).

The players then have seven minutes to put a word in each box. The word in the box must fit the category above it and begin with the letter on the left of it.

At the end of seven minutes, players stop writing and take turns reading their words in the first box. Each player scores his own paper. Zero points are given for a blank box. One point is given if another person had the same word, and two points are given if the word is unique. A numeral is written in the box for the score; this procedure is followed for each box. The points are then totaled for each box. There is a maximum of 50 points.

The game is repeated and points are accumulated; the highest scorer wins.

Total Points: 32	FOOD	MUSICAL INSTRU- MENTS	ANIMALS	FLOWERS	SPORTS
G	1 grapes	1 guitar	2 giraffe	1 geranium	0 _____
R	2 rhubarb	0 _____	1 rabbit	1 rose	2 rugby
A	1 apple	2 autoharp	2 alligator	0 _____	2 alligator wrestling
N	2 navy beans	0 _____	2 night hawk	2 narcissus	0 _____
T	2 toast	1 trombone	2 turtle	2 tea rose	1 tennis

Purpose or Benefit

"Categories" is a creative thinking game. It encourages quick thinking and some strategy in word choice.

Dots and Lines

Number of Players: 2-5

Length of Time: 5-20 minutes

Materials: Pencil
Paper

Object of the Game: To draw the last possible line.

To Play:

Five or six well-spaced dots are marked. By turn, each player connects a dot with another dot or brings the line back to the same dot and marks the line with an additional dot. No new line drawn may cross any existing lines. It must end only at a dot with no more than *two* lines connected to it already.

The player to draw the last line wins.

Variation:

For a greater challenge, more initial dots are marked.

Comments:

If more than two or three play, it is best to play several games, with each player taking a turn at drawing the first line.

Purpose or Benefit

This game is easy to learn and needs few materials, yet it is highly challenging.

Name the States

Number of Players:	2-20
Length of Time:	10-30 minutes
Materials:	Paper Pens and pencils Writing surfaces Clock or watch
Object of the Game:	To remember and write down more states than anyone else.

To Play:

Each player is given a piece of paper, a pen or pencil, and a writing surface. One person is designated as the timekeeper.

At a signal from the timekeeper, each player writes the names of as many of the fifty United States as he can.

The timekeeper lets the other players know when five minutes are up, and all must stop writing. Each player counts the number of states he has written down.

The players take turns announcing how many states they have, and reading their lists to the rest of the group. The one who has the most states written is the winner.

Variations:

1. Each player is given a list of all fifty states and tries to name their capital cities.

2. The players try to recall the names of countries.

3. The players, given a list of countries, try to name their capital cities.

Purpose or Benefit

"Name the States" encourages quick thinking, exercises the memory, and increases knowledge of geography.

Quiet Circle Games

Pass Around the Ring

Number of Players:	5-20
Length of Time:	15-45 minutes
Material:	A ring or very small object
Object of the Game:	To give the ring away without anyone else knowing.

To Play:

Everyone sits in a circle. One person stands in the center with the ring.

The person with the ring walks from one person to the next around the circle and pretends to give the ring to each person. He can give it to anyone, or he can keep it himself. He then asks someone in the circle to guess who has it.

If that person guesses correctly, the person who started with the ring remains in the center and repeats the process. If the person guesses wrong, he is given the ring and becomes the "ring-passer."

Purpose or Benefit

"Pass Around the Ring" is a good icebreaker and challenges the players' perceptiveness.

Red-Handed

Number of Players: 5-15

Length of Time: 15-30 minutes

Material: A marble, stone, or other small object

Object of the Game: To catch the person holding the marble.

To Play:

One person is chosen as "it." The other players gather in a circle around "it." The player who is "it" closes his eyes and the others start passing the marble (or other small concealable object) from person to person.

The best method of passing is to hold the object in one fist, palm down and drop it into the open palm of another player. Fake passes are an important part of the game.

"It" opens his eyes and tries to guess who has the marble, which he indicates by tapping the person's fist. The marble can be continually passed around right under "it's" nose.

The person who is caught is the new "it." If "it" fails to catch someone after a certain time limit, he designates a player to replace him.

Purpose or Benefit

This game encourages cooperation and can be played by all ages.

Ring on a String

Number of Players:	4-15
Length of Time:	10-30 minutes
Materials:	A very long piece of rope, twine, yarn or string A ring or other small object which can be "strung" on the string. With small children, the best choice is an object slightly larger than a ring, yet one that can be concealed in their hands.
Object of the Game:	For "it": to catch the ring as it is being passed between players. For the players in the circle: to pass the ring to one another on the string, concealing the ring so "it" cannot detect it.

To Play:

The players stand in a circle, arms' length away from each other, with "it" in the center. A string, long enough to extend easily around the circle (with a little slack), is sent around the circle with each player holding onto it with both hands. A ring is strung on the string, concealed under one of the player's hands.

The ring is set in motion between players, who must keep it moving continually. The ring is passed along and the players try to conceal it from "it"; he watches alertly to catch a glimpse of the ring as it is passed along.

When "it" catches a player with the ring, the player becomes "it."

Purpose or Benefit

"Ring on a String" does not require special skill, and children, or adults and children, can play it together.

Telephone

Number of Players:	5-15
Length of Time:	10-30 minutes
Object of the Game:	To see how intact a sentence will remain after being whispered from person to person.

To Play:

The players sit in a circle and everyone agrees who will start the sentence. The player starting whispers a sentence to the player next to him, who in turn repeats the sentence to the player next to *him*.

The retelling continues around the circle. Each player may whisper the sentence only once. The last person says the sentence aloud.

The game is repeated until each player is given a chance to start a sentence.

Purpose or Benefit

"Telephone" is a good game for groups of all ages. It is a good experience in communication.

MISCELLANEOUS

A game book would not be complete without a "miscellaneous" section as a catch-all for those great games which do not fit into any broad category. "Miscellaneous" is subdivided into:

> Trip Games
> Card Games
> A Homemade Board Game
> Party Games
> Traveling Games

Many of the games throughout the book could be played in a car or on a trip, but the *trip games* are specifically created for that purpose.

No attempt has been made in this book to include all the many *card games*. The games here are more unusual, entertaining, or exciting than standard traditional card games.

Many games in this book are good *party games*; however, those in this section are designed specifically for parties.

Traveling games are those in which players must travel to various places to play the game.

Alphabet Travel Game

Number of Players: 2-10

Length of Time: 15 minutes to 2 hours

Playing Site: Traveling in a bus or car, preferably on a longer trip

Object of the Game: To be the first player to find all the letters in the alphabet.

To Play:

Each player must try to find all the letters of the alphabet *in order* (A-Z) on road signs, license plates, store fronts, etc. The player who finds the "Z" first wins.

Variations:

1. Instead of a race, this game can be played as a group with one player finding the A, the next player finding the B, and so on. The group tries to find the alphabet in a certain amount of time or people time themselves each game, trying to beat their own records.

2. Players try to find *objects* beginning with the letter they are looking for. For example, if a player is on the letter "c" and sees a cow, he would announce "C, cow." He would receive credit for that letter and also make that particular object inaccessible for others to use. Thus, when someone else is on the letter "c," for example, he must find a car, coffee sign, camel (!), or some other object that begins with "c." The first person to complete the alphabet wins.

3. Players find numbers in sequential order instead of letters.

Comments:

Some letters are more difficult to find than others, such as "J," "Q", "X," "Z," and may be excluded from the game if the players wish.

Purpose or Benefit

"Alphabet Travel Game" is a good educational game for children who have just learned their alphabet and/or numbers. It is also a pleasant way to pass the time in a car without requiring the complete attention of the participants—they are still free to talk and enjoy one another while watching for letters.

License Plate Bingo

Number of Players: 3-10

Length of Time: 20-60 minutes

Materials: "Bingo" cards
Pencils

Playing Site: Traveling in a bus or car, preferably on a longer trip

Preparation: Bingo cards are made in advance by dividing plain sheets of paper into grids of 25 1" squares, 5 across and 5 down. Each square is marked with a two-digit number selected randomly from 00 to 99. However, the center box is marked "FREE" and is not assigned a number.

Object of the Game: To be the first player to "Bingo" by filling in 5 boxes on his card which form a straight line vertically, horizontally, or diagonally.

To Play:

One player is chosen to be referee. The referee hands out the bingo cards, one per player. As cars pass, the referee calls out the last two digits of their license plate numbers. Each two-digit number called is recorded separately by the referee.

As the referee calls a number, each player checks his Bingo card to see if that two-digit number is in one of his squares. If it is, he crosses out that square. When a player is able to cross out 5 squares which form a line vertically, horizontally, or diagonally he calls, "Bingo!" At this the game stops and the referee then double-checks the Bingo by checking each number in the squares forming the Bingo against the list he has been keeping of all numbers which he called. Note that all players may use the "FREE" square as a part of their sequences. If the Bingo called is valid, the player whose card formed the Bingo is the winner. If a mistake has been made, the game continues until a valid Bingo is formed.

Comment:

Added excitement can be provided by promising a small prize to the winner.

Purpose or Benefit

"License Plate Bingo" is a good game with which to pass time while traveling. It gives interest and excitement to a time which otherwise might be boring and tiring.

Card Games

Blind Folly

Number of Players:	4
Length of Time:	15-30 minutes
Material:	Deck of Rook ® cards
Special Requirement:	Players should know how to play the Rook "Regular Game."
Preparation:	The deck of cards is prepared as for the Rook "Regular Game."
Object of the Game:	To take three or more tricks on as many bids as possible.

To Play:

The cards are dealt as if to play the Rook "Regular Game." However, instead of looking at their own cards, players turn their hands so that all players may see them except themselves.

Play then proceeds as in the "Regular Game," except that, of course, no one knows what he himself is playing.

Comment:

Partners should not let each other know when the other starts to make a poor choice from his hand.

Purpose or Benefit

"Blind Folly" is humorous, but not challenging, since players can make no intelligent decisions. It provides light entertainment.

Low Joe

Number of Players: 4-8

Length of Time: 10-30 minutes

Materials: Deck of Rook ® cards
                         Chips or other suitable tokens

Object of the Game: To avoid holding the lowest card.

To Play:

Each player begins with three chips.

One card is dealt to each player, face down. The deck remains face down. Play begins at the dealer's left and continues clockwise. Each player in turn observes the face of his card. If it is a 14, he puts it face-up in front of him. If he does not have a 14, but thinks that his card will probably not be the lowest one dealt, he may say "stand," keeping his card face down. If a player thinks that his card is dangerously low, he may swap cards with the player on his left. When it is the dealer's turn, if he chooses to swap, he does so with the top card of the deck.

All players then turn their cards face-up. The player with the lowest card must put a chip into the "kitty." If cards of equal numbers are exposed, they rank in this order: black, red, green, yellow, with black as the highest.

The play is repeated, rotating the deal, until only one person has any chips. He is the winner.

Comments:

Children enjoy "Low Joe" especially if the kitty is made up of an edible treat instead of chips.

Purpose or Benefit

"Low Joe" requires little skill, but the suspense is exciting.

I Doubt It

Number of Players:	5-9
Length of Time:	30-90 minutes
Material:	Deck of Rook ® cards
Object of the Game:	To be the first player to run out of cards.

To Play:

All cards are dealt, and players study their hands. The player to the dealer's left places one, two, three or four cards face down in front of him and identifies them as same-number cards—for instance, "three Eights." The player to his left then must introduce cards in like manner of the next number up. Each player in turn does likewise. For example, if player A announced, "Two Fives," player B would then have to announce one to four Sixes.

Players have the option of "deceiving their opponents." In other words, the cards played may not be as they were identified. If someone suspects that another player has done this, he may say, "I doubt it," immediately after the play. At that point, the player accused must expose his cards. If he has been dishonest, he must add all the face-down cards on the table to his hand. If the *accuser* is wrong, he must take the cards.

Play continues until one player runs out of cards, and wins. His last play should be an authentic one, for he will certainly be challenged in a final effort by his opponents.

Purpose or Benefit

"I Doubt It" requires little skill, yet is challenging in that it requires discretion and some insight into what the other players are thinking.

Snap

Number of Players: 2-6

Length of Time: 15-45 minutes

Material: Deck of Rook ® cards

Object of the Game: To gain all of the cards.

To Play:

The cards are equally distributed to the players. Each player places his cards face down, unseen, in a pile in front of him.

The players take turns turning up the top cards of their piles, so that a pile of face-up cards gradually accumulates in front of each player. All players watch for a card to be turned up that matches the number of any of the top face-up cards. The first one to say "Snap" when this happens wins both of the piles that have the matching top cards. These are added to his face-down cards.

If two players tie in saying "Snap," the two matching piles are put in the middle and the game continues until a third matching number is turned up. The first player to say "Snapee," or, "Snap pool," then wins the three piles with the matching cards. If two people are tied again, the third pile is also placed in the middle. When the fourth matching number is turned up, the first player to say "Snapeewee" wins all four piles.

When a player has turned up all of his face-down cards, he continues to play by turning his face-up cards over and using them.

A player is eliminated when all of his cards have been captured.

The last player who captures all of the cards is the winner.

Purpose or Benefit

Attentiveness is required for success at "Snap." It is an ideal game to play when a complete deck is not available, since a few cards missing will have little effect on the game.

Snip, Snap, Snorem!

Number of Players: 3-6

Length of Time: 10-20 minutes

Material: Deck of Rook ® cards

Object of the Game: To be the first to get rid of one's cards.

To Play:

The cards are dealt out to the players, and each player looks at his own cards. The player to the left of the dealer lays down any card face up on the table. The second player, if he has a same number card, lays it down face up and says, "Snip." If he does not have a matching card, he passes. The next player to have another card that matches says "Snap" as he lays it down. The player who has the fourth matching card says "Snorem" as he lays it down, and begins the next round by laying another card face up on the table.

If a player is holding two matching cards, he plays them one at a time in two separate turns.

The first to get rid of all of his cards is the winner.

Purpose or Benefit

"Snip, Snap, Snorem" is simple, but generates constant activity. Children will enjoy it because they will have plenty of opportunity to participate.

Spoons

Number of Players:	3-10
Length of Time:	30-90 minutes
Materials:	One deck of Rook ® cards One less spoon than the total number of players (e.g., for 4 players, 3 spoons)
Playing Site:	A table and chairs to accommodate all players
Object of the Game:	To avoid being the player without a spoon at the end of each round.

To Play:

Spoons need to be placed in an orderly fashion, central to all players.

The dealer deals out four cards to each player and then places the deck face down near him. He picks up the top card and either adds it to his hand and discards another card, or simply discards the card he has just drawn. He continues through the rest of the deck in the same way, one card at a time. The player to his left draws cards from the dealer's discard pile in the same way, and so on around the circle. Players do not take turns, but begin drawing and discarding as soon as cards are available to them.

This process continues until one person gets four of a number. That person then grabs a spoon. Immediately, all the other players attempt to take a spoon. The player without a spoon loses the round. Additional rounds are played rotating the deal.

Scoring is as follows: For each loss, the player gets one letter of the word "spoons." After his first loss, he receives "s," after the second "p," and so on. When a player spells "spoons," he is out of the game. To continue playing after a player goes out, remove one of the spoons. The game continues until all players but one have spelled "spoons." The player who has not spelled "spoons" at the end wins.

Variations:

1. Other words instead of "spoons" may be used to keep score.

The person with the fewest letters after a certain amount of time wins.

2. Players are penalized by receiving a letter if they grab a spoon before someone with four of a number does.

3. The number of cards in the deck may be reduced. If, for example, there are five people playing, the cards being used may be limited to 2, 3, 4, 5 and 6 in every color. This will generally result in a quicker game.

Comments:

It may be advisable to use old or nonvaluable cards and spoons, as their condition may be worsened by the end of the game.

A player may pretend to reach for a spoon to fool the other players.

With extra large groups it may be necessary to use two decks of Rook cards.

This game can be rather loud and is very exciting.

Purpose or Benefit

"Spoons" generates a high level of speed and excitement, yet can be learned quickly and requires no particular card skill.

A Homemade Board Game

Race to the Inn

Number of Players:	3-6
Length of Time:	20-60 minutes
Materials:	1 die
	Diagram of course to be run
	(see diagram)
	Coins or chips
	Playing tokens
	Paper
	Pencil

Preparation: On a piece of paper or cardboard a
diagram is drawn of 60-80 steps from
"home" to "inn."

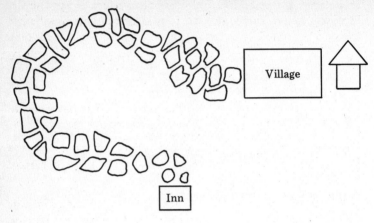

Object of the Game: To be the first to get back to the village.

To Play:

To complete the race, players need to move from the village to
the inn, and back to the village two times. To make progress,
each player in turn rolls the die and advances as indicated below. More than one player may occupy a space with no penalty to either for most of the game. A "taba" is a unit of exchange represented by a coin or chip given the player entitled
to it.

Player rolls:
   1—Receives a taba and rolls again
   2—Moves two spaces
   3—Moves three spaces and rolls again
   4—Receives a taba
   5—Moves one space and rolls again
   6—Moves six spaces and rolls again

Players are represented by playing tokens which are placed in
the village to begin the game. In order to advance from the village, a player must first roll a number entitling him to a taba.
He exchanges this taba to be able to leave the village.

To be admitted to the Inn, a player must roll the die to advance the exact number of spaces he is away from the Inn. Or,

if he rolls short, he can make up the difference by exchanging a taba for every space he wishes to move.

In order to leave the Inn and begin the return trip to the village, four tabas are required. A player may pay them if he has them, or wait till he rolls them on his turns. The player may keep track of any advancing rolls he tosses while attempting to accumulate tabas, and use them at other points in the game when he rolls nonadvancing numbers.

Players return to the village in the same manner they went. In order to leave the village again, two tabas are required.

On their second journey to the Inn, players move *double* the number indicated on the key. To leave the inn the second time, 10 tabas are required.

When players are on their final "home stretch," they continue to move at double speed. In addition, any players they land on are eliminated from the game.

The first player to arrive safely home on the second trip wins. The other players continue attempting to finish the race without being eliminated by the others.

Purpose or Benefit

"Race to the Inn" is a board game that is easy to make and play.

Party Games

Balloon Game

Number of Players:	4
Length of Time:	5-20 minutes
Materials:	Balloons (all the same size)—about 20 for each person playing
Playing Site:	A moderately large open area
Preparation:	All the balloons must be blown up in advance.

Object of the Game: To see how many balloons one person can hold using his arms, legs, chin, etc.

To Play:

All the balloons are placed on the floor in the center of the room, with players in a circle around them. At the referee's signal, all the players simultaneously start picking up balloons, attempting to hold as many at once as possible with the various parts of their body, and remain standing.

At the end of the time limit, the referee signals everyone to stop. The person holding the most balloons is the winner.

Comment:

With larger groups, depending on room size and number of balloons, it may be easier to have players go in groups of two to six, rather than all at once.

Purpose or Benefit

The "Balloon Game" is an especially good game for children's parties, although people of any age enjoy it.

Find the Pins in the Rice

Number of Players: 3-12

Length of Time: 10-30 minutes

Materials: Small mixing bowl
20-30 very small safety pins, closed
Uncooked long-grain rice
Blindfold
Watch with second hand
Paper
Pencils

Preparation: The bowl is half-filled with rice and the safety pins are mixed into it.

Object of the Game: To be the one who finds the most pins in the rice.

To Play:

A player is appointed as timekeeper.

One player at a time is blindfolded. The bowl of rice is placed in front of him. When the timekeeper signals to begin, the player uses one hand to find the pins mixed in with the rice and removes them as he does so. The player must stop when the timekeeper indicates that one minute has passed.

The pins removed are counted and then mixed back into the rice for the next player. The one who is able to find the most safety pins is the winner.

Purpose or Benefit

"Find the Pins in the Rice" tests one's sense of touch.

Pass the Parcel

Number of Players:	5-20
Length of Time:	5-15 minutes
Materials:	Small, well-wrapped prize Piano or record player and record
Preparation:	The prize is wrapped in several layers of paper. Music is prepared for use.
Object of the Game:	To be the one who unwraps the last bit of wrapping.

To Play:

One person plays the piano or record. Players sit in a circle, each passing the parcel to the player on his left. When the music stops, whoever has the parcel in his hand begins to unwrap it, until the music begins when he must pass it on. Whoever finishes the unwrapping keeps the prize.

Comments:

If players tend to hang onto the parcel, instead of quickly passing it on while the music is playing, then a penalty may be imposed for holding the unwrapped prize in one's hands.

More than one prize can be used so several players can win.

Purpose or Benefit

A popular party game that is an easy way to win a prize.

Spider Web

Number of Players:	3-10
Length of Time:	30-60 minutes
Materials:	Heavy string or thin rope Prizes
Playing Site:	A room cleared of breakable objects
Preparation:	String is cut into several *long* pieces of equal length. All strings start at a common point, such as the door to the room. One piece at a time, string is woven around the room, getting entangled with chair legs, tables, and other pieces of string. Each string ends with a prize tied to it. When done, the "web" should weave all over the room, but without tight knots.
Object of the Game:	To be the first to reach a prize.

To Play:

Players are each assigned one string. At the command "Go!" all begin to untangle the "web," winding their respective strings into balls as they go. The first player to wind all of his string into a ball and reach his prize wins. However, all players continue to follow their strings to their individual prizes.

Comments:

The "web" is almost as much fun to make as it is to untangle. Preparing the room is best done by two or three people together.

This game can be simple or very demanding depending upon how many players are involved and how entangled the web is.

Purpose or Benefit

Patience and cooperation are developed by players of "Spider Web."

Traveling Games

Road Rally

Number of Players:	2-24
Length of Time:	1-4 hours
Materials:	Sufficient number of cars to carry the teams Envelopes and cards for clues to be written on Bibles and maps for each team
Playing Site:	A familiar locale
Preparation:	Clues are prepared as follows: a clue (often a scripture verse) is written on the outside of each clue envelope. The clue should somehow direct the team to the place where the next clue envelope is hidden. (For scriptural clues, all players should use the same translation of the Bible.) The solution is written on a card and placed inside each envelope so the teams can refer to these as a last resort.
	The clues, except for the first one, are then distributed and hidden around town—friends' homes are good locations. It is best to have a different

route for each team, so that they can not follow each other.

Four to ten different clues are written for each team, making sure the teams have an equal number of clues to decipher *and* about the same distance to travel in the course of the rally.

Object of the Game: To be the first team to complete the course and look at the fewest solutions to the clues.

To Play:

Participants are divided into teams of four to six people. Each team must have a car. The driver of the car for each team is given the first clue envelope. Each team works together to decipher its clue, which will lead them to clue #2. Clue #2 will lead them to clue #3, and so on. The last clue leads home.

Variations:

1. Rather than starting with one clue only, all the clues may be given at once. Having them all, each team can plot its own course in the most efficient way. At each stop-off point a card is collected to verify that they have successfully figured out the clue.

2. Instead of placing the solutions to the clues inside the envelopes, each team is given a telephone number which can be called if unable to figure out a clue. The person being reached by phone gives additional clues to help them discover the answer.

3. When directed to the home of someone known to the participants, they sing a song for them.

4. "Road Rally" can be played without cars in a confined area, a park, or even indoors, if the mayhem is bearable and the group small.

5. The first team to reach home may receive a prize.

Comments:

If some players are not familiar with the area in which the game is being played, they may easily become lost. To remedy this possibility, the teams can be given a phone number which they may call for directions.

A nice prize for the first team home is to allow them the privilege of preparing and serving a snack for the losers when they arrive.

Purpose or Benefit

These rallies, or "treasure hunts," provide much exciting interaction within the teams as players try to decipher the clues. If scriptural clues are used, participants' knowledge of the Bible will be increased by playing "Road Rally."

Scavenger Hunt

Number of Players:　4-40

Length of Time:　1-3 hours

Materials:　List of articles
Paper bag for each team, large enough to hold all the items
Car for each team if they are to travel farther than walking distance

Preparation:　Prepare a list of articles for each team to find. The lists may or may not be identical, but must be equal in length. A sample list could be:
　An empty spool of thread
　An old sock
　A broken pencil
　A graham cracker
　An autographed Q-tip
　A whisker from a beard
　A comic book
　A piece of green construction paper

Object of the Game:　To collect the greatest number of items on the list within the allotted time.

To Play:

The group is divided into teams. Teams of four or five are ideal.

The teams all depart at the same time, either on foot or in cars. They go to neighbors' homes, or homes of friends, to secure the listed items.

The teams return home when they either: (1) have collected all the items, or (2) run out of time, whichever comes first. The first team that returns with the items, or the team that finds the most in the allotted time, wins.

Comment:

If specific homes of friends are going to be visited, it is advisable to call them in advance to see if anyone will be home and if it will be all right to call on them. The teams are told which homes to visit.

Purpose or Benefit

The teamwork involved in "Scavenger Hunt" produces a sense of unity. This game also provides much time for fellowship in small groups, as the teams travel together to their destinations. When homes of friends are visited for help in acquiring the items, the amount of fellowship and relationship-building increases.

FAMILY AND FELLOWSHIP ACTIVITIES

This section of *Games* is provided as a resource for families and groups of Christians who plan times of fellowship. In addition to playing the games detailed in the first portion of this book, God's people will find the activities described in this section to be enjoyable recreation.

Obviously, this list is not exhaustive; families or Christian groups will creatively add many ideas as they brainstorm other ways of spending time together. Also, not everything mentioned will appeal to or be workable for every family or group. Some activities may be more appropriate for groups of adults; others, for adults and children.

Quiet Evenings at Home

Games—Traditional and Creative

Various *board* or *card* games can be played. The host can provide a variety or each person can bring their favorite board game or introduce a favorite card game.

Board or card games can be played *noncompetitively*—after each turn or two, the players rotate one position.

Games from this book can be played.

A *card house* can be constructed by arranging playing cards appropriately.

A *backwards spelling bee* is accomplished by requiring participants to spell words backwards.

Quiz books: Books with quiz questions can be used for competition. The reader may wish to devise a point system for correct answers given and reward winners accordingly.

Show Time

Home movies, slides from a trip, or a movie from a public library may be shown.

A good *movie on TV*, with popcorn, is also enjoyable.

Performing

Talent show—Acts are prepared and presented.

Music night—Each person plays a musical instrument, to contribute to a group ensemble. If there is a shortage of musical instruments or musicians, or if preferred, kazoos may be substituted for instruments.

Sing-alongs—All gather around a piano to sing hymns, old favorite folk songs, or Christmas carols.

Individuals take turns teaching the group a favorite song.

Dance—A group learns and does Hebrew or other folk

dances. Spontaneous interpretative dancing is done to Christian music.

Stories

Storytelling—Individuals take turns telling stories, jokes, or recounting humorous incidents (enjoyable before a roaring fire).

Story reading—Individuals take turns reading from a short book or story. Children's books are good for this.

Poetry reading—Each person is given a poetry book and all take turns selecting a poem and reading it aloud. It is best to keep the poems under a certain length.

Individual Expression

Discussing scripture—After a scripture is selected and read, the group separates for individual meditation. When the group gathers again, all share what the passage means to them and how they can apply it.

Telling about ourselves—Each person recounts a *personal experience* on a given topic, such as "My most memorable birthday (or Christmas)," "My high school years," "My most embarrassing experience," etc.

Each person brings a *photograph* of himself at an early age and uses it to tell something about his life.

Each person presents his *testimony*—how he came to know the Lord.

The group separates so that each person can write his own personal *"gospel"* about his life with the Lord. Then all read what they have written.

One person prepares and relates his *life story*. Childhood photographs, scrapbooks, demonstrations, etc., will make such a presentation more lively.

Edification Night/Praise Time

In some orderly way, everyone comments on the strengths, qualities, gifts, and other positive things he sees in the others.

Tape Listening

Speakers recorded on cassette tapes provide for either serious or humorous listening.

Sewing

Everyone works on individual sewing projects or mending (for others, as well as for themselves).

Food Preparation

Many kinds of fun foods can be cooperatively prepared (e.g., homemade ice cream).

Crafts

Candles

Banners

Posters

Greeting cards

Stationery

Christmas ornaments

Montage

Macrame

Carpentry

Furniture building

Metal work

Decoupage

Crocheting

Knitting

Needlecraft

Soap carving (e.g., making a nativity scene)

The enjoyment of these activities may be enhanced by having an experienced person demonstrate and teach the other participants.

Any of the above can be made as gifts and then exchanged.

Creative-Giving Night

Participants are divided into several smaller groups. Each group thinks of something to do or make for the rest of the group. Examples: cook a treat, perform a skit, make a banner, sing a song, mend clothes, make up a game—anything to serve the others. At the end of the evening each group presents to the others what it has done.

Celebrations and Special Dinners

"Deck the Halls" Night

Everyone is involved in some way in preparing the house for Christmas. This could include: making decorations, trimming the tree, decorating the house with pine boughs, constructing a nativity scene, baking, singing Christmas carols, etc.

Old-fashioned Birthday Party

A birthday is celebrated as children do, with cake and ice cream, "pin-the-tail-on-the-donkey," funny hats, and other trimmings.

Ethnic Dinner

A country or certain ethnic group is selected as a theme. Appropriate food is served for dinner. Special music, clothes, and dancing add to the experience, as well as slides or a movie on the particular country.

Strawberry Shortcake Festival

(Or any other fruit in season) Small groups are formed, appropriate to the magnitude of their task, to pick the strawberries, clean them, make or bring ice cream, and bake shortcake.

Progressive Dinner

A different home is visited for each course of a meal. If the group is large, it can be divided into small groups, which rotate among the hosts' homes until they have partaken of every course. The small groups may then rendezvous at a larger location for dessert.

Outings

Outdoor

A bonfire
A picnic
A corn roast
Kite-flying
Canoeing
Tobogganing
A zoo
A cider mill
A museum
A park
An ethnic festival—when available
A hike*
A hayride

*Especially good places to go for hikes are gardens, parks, arboretums, and college campuses.

Performances

Christian coffeehouses
Concerts
Plays
Movies
Planetarium
Travelogues
High school football games
Christian speakers

Sports

Badminton	Horseshoes
Basketball	Ice Skating
Bicycling	Miniature Golf
Bowling	Roller Skating
Croquet	Swimming
Four Square	Table Tennis
Frisbee	Volleyball

Besides participatory sports, an enjoyable activity may be attending a spectator sporting event together.

Visiting

Visit homes of friends, relatives, other families in your church or fellowship group.

Carolling or serenading—friends, neighborhood homes, or nursing homes may be serenaded.

CHILDREN'S GAMES AND ACTIVITY IDEAS

Here is a valuable resource for those who plan and/or conduct activities for children. The ideas and events in this section were used with children in kindergarten through sixth grade. However, many of the activities can be easily adapted for preschool children or teenagers.

All of these activities have been tested; advice and practical wisdom is offered on how to make them work best with different age groups. After each activity was conducted, it was evaluated—suggestions for improvement and greater success are included.

Our Youth Activities program is divided by sex and age group. We have found these divisions helpful so that children of common interests and abilities do things together. We have tried grouping different grades together and have found the below most successful.

> K-1 Boys
> K-1 Girls
> 2-3 Boys
> 2-3 Girls
> 4-6 Boys
> 4-6 Girls

Outdoor Activities

Games and Sports

Children of all ages enjoy outdoor games and sports. With a little creativity, the following can be adapted to a variety of age groups. Younger children have a shorter attention span, so it is helpful to plan to keep them active and involved at all times. Regardless of the type of group, the participation of many interested adults is a key to success, and bad weather plans should never be neglected!

1. *Kickball.*

2. *Football*: Smaller balls are available and the rules can be modified for younger children (e.g., two-handed touch, no passing, no kicking, etc.).

3. *Baseball.*

4. *Soccer*: Many times it is helpful to have warm-up drills first

5. *Badminton.*

6. *Volleyball.*

7. *Dodgeball.*

8. *Roller skating.*

9. *Ice skating.*

10. *Canoeing*: For older boys especially, this activity can be extended into an all-day adventure or overnight trip. It's always fun to invite fathers to come along! If possible, stopping to explore the shore along the way makes the trip much more interesting.

11. *Swimming:* Especially with younger children, a good adult-to-child ratio is helpful. Come prepared with ideas of games to play in the water, as well as some balls or water toys.

12. *Bowling.*

13. *Croquet.*

14. *Fishing*: Boys especially enjoy this, and if the lake or river is well stocked with fish, it can be an exciting activity.

15. *"Traditional" games*: "Mother May I"; "Hot or Cold"; "Hopscotch"; relay races. Many other games are described in this book. These activities can always be "spiced up" by entitling your event "Outdoor Games Day" or by giving it a theme of some kind.

16. *Miniature golf.*

17. *Jump rope*: This traditional activity always has great appeal to girls, and we have invented some Christian words to use in place of other well-known verses.

> Down in the valley, where the green grass grows.
> There stood a little sheep lost and alone.
> Along came the shepherd to take her back home.
> How many sheep rejoiced with her? 1-2-3. . . .

> Jesus walked the ocean.
> Jesus calmed the sea.
> Jesus gave me new life,
> When He died for me.
> How many blessings did I receive? 1-2-3. . . .

Other Activities

There is no end to the possible ways of having fun with children in the out-of-doors! Younger children are thrilled with spontaneous discoveries and a creative adult can make great use of unusual trees, birds, mud puddles, and so on.

1. *"Mud day"*: Younger boys always enjoy the chance to build mud castles, dams, bridges, throw stones into a river, find snails, etc., and this interest can be channeled into a fun activity. Arrange ahead of time for a place to wash up, and for an extra change of clothing.

2. *Tracking*: Older children enjoy finding animal tracks and trying to find their "owners." A variation that works especially well with younger children is to have an adult leave clues or tracks throughout the woods, or in the snow, and have the children track this "mysterious beast." Inventing a name for the "animal" adds to the excitement, and allowing the children to take turns leading the group keeps interest high.

3. *Treasure hunt*: Similar to the above activity, but a special

prize at the end is the goal. Clues can be given in a variety of ways—posted on trees throughout the woods, hidden in various spots in a field, and so on. The clues can be in the form of riddles, or can indicate a task to be performed by the group (e.g., sing a song or do a simple skit) in order to earn their next clue. It keeps interest high if the groups are small and the "treasure" appealing.

4. *Scavenger hunt.*

5. *Jump in leaves*: An attractive, yet simple, variation is to pile the leaves at the foot of a slide and let the children slide into them.

6. *Feed animals*: Ducks at a pond or animals in a zoo.

7. *Kite-flying*: All ages enjoy this, though younger children have a much shorter attention span. Good weather and experienced helpers are invaluable to this activity!

8. *A walk down a frozen river.* (Be sure it's frozen!)

9. *Nature hike*: Hikes can be enhanced in a variety of ways. For example, children love to take photographs and a polaroid camera is a great asset to any hike.

10. *Bird-watching*: Small groups of older children are best for this activity. Binoculars, a field guide, and interested adults will make this venture a success.

11. *Winter picnic*: Depending on the particular children, a picnic out in the snow can be a memorable adventure.

12. *Snow activities*: Sledding, tobogganing, snowball fights, building snow forts, "garbage bagging" (cutting out arm and leg holes in large plastic garbage bags and sliding down a hill is great fun), using inner tubes to slide down a hill. These are but a few possibilities for fun in the snow. If a large group is sledding, setting up a "traffic flow" pattern on the hills avoids many problems.

13. *Visit a farm.*

14. *Camping*: The location and length of time varies according to age groups of children, yet even young children enjoy sleeping in a tent in the backyard. This is an activity requiring a good deal of planning.

15. *Hayride*: A hayride well-planned with songs and games is

a great activity. Combine it with a hot dog roast, or cider and donuts.

16. *Apple-picking*: This can be stretched into two activities by baking something with the apples the children pick.

17. *Outdoor cooking*: Many skills can be taught in this activity. Fire-building, camp-menu planning, and so on. It's helpful to have a fire prepared well in advance so it is hot enough to cook on when it is time.

18. *Bonfire/campfire*: All children love to be around bonfires and will enjoy it if it is well planned with a variety of songs and activities.

19. *Bike hike*: This can be a real adventure for a group of children, especially if the destination is enticing (e.g., a lake for swimming or a park for a picnic). It works best to have small groups stick together with an adult and have an adult follow the group in a van or station wagon stocked with bicycle parts, a first-aid kit, water, tools, etc. It is important to test the route in advance and give clear directions to each group.

    Variation: Have a "tricycle hike" for younger children. You can visit a nearby park, or just go around the neighborhood, and return for a picnic.

20. *Bus ride*: Younger children especially enjoy riding city buses. You may be provided with free bus passes if you call ahead and explain your purpose. Your destination can be anywhere!

21. *Water-balloon toss.*

22. *Go as a group to see an athletic event*—professional, college, or high school

23. *Play on toys at a park*: Younger children can derive hours of pleasure from swings, slides, monkey bars, and other equipment at a local playground.

24. *Airport tour*: This is interesting, but should be kept "short and sweet" to maintain excitement. The ride to and from the airport can be a time for making paper airplanes, singing "airplane" songs, and so on.

25. *Sidewalk chalk painting.*

26. *Visit the county fair.*

27. *Tour a nearby town*: Visit the library, feed the ducks, go to the ice cream parlor, see historical sites, etc.

28. *Pick wild flowers.*

Indoor Activities

Games, crafts, field trips, and parties are activities antici-pated by all children, and there are infinite combinations and variations of such events. Remember that children have high energy levels and the most successful games and activities are ones that *keep moving.*

Young children greatly enjoy unstructured free play as part of their time together; this can be very rewarding for adults that involve themselves in such times. Keep in mind that even old games can create high interest if given a new name, or a new twist.

1. Many games described in other sections of this book are great for children. Some favorites are "Dr. Tangle," "Poof Ball," and "Machine Charades."

2. *Board games*: Anticipation is built if each child brings his favorite game.

3. *Movies*: Easily acquired from a public library, movies are always entertaining. It is important to preview unfamiliar films. *Variation*: During the summer, show the movie out-side, against the wall of a house or garage.

4. *Slides*: These are especially interesting if you take slides of various activities the children participate in.

5. *Tea party*: Younger girls especially enjoy dressing up in fancy clothes, setting the table with good teacups, silver-ware, tablecloth, and centerpiece, and having special food. All should use their best manners—this could be a great opportunity to teach these!

6. *"Indoor Olympics"*: Olympic events can be adapted to the indoors. For instance, the javelin throw becomes a toothpick throw against a target on the wall. Balloons are used for the shotput. The high jump consists of jumping up and down saying "high" and seeing who can last the longest.

7. *Read or tell a story* and have the children act it out. *Variation*: Use the children's names and familiar places and events in the story.

8. *"Pretend"*: The children can act out what it's like to be popcorn-popping, bubbles-bursting, and so on.

9. *Make human pyramids.*

10. *Tell favorite jokes or riddles.*

11. *Play card games.*

12. *Trade lunches or snacks* prepared ahead of time by each child.

13. *Log book*: Have the children write or draw what they did at the activity. This can be done at each activity and by a different child or children at each event. Make it a "special" task.

14. *Percussion jam*: Using cowbells, wood blocks, tambourines, etc., the children can play spontaneously for a while and then organize for a "music lesson."

15. *"Building day"*: Younger boys enjoy using blocks—Lincoln logs, Lego blocks, and other materials—to construct buildings or whole towns.

16. *Skits*: Especially popular with 8-12-year-old girls, there are many ways to perform skits. A particularly successful variation is "Paper-Bag Skits" (see page 129).

17. *Crafts night*: Each child brings a craft project and works on it in a group setting. Older girls often enjoy this.

18. *Police/Fire station tour*: Children love these trips, especially if they get to participate in activities such as finger printing.

19. *Pet store tour*: A store with a great variety of unusual animals is an irresistible attraction for children!

20. *"Skills night"*: Children can be taught a variety of useful skills such as making a bed, chopping wood, setting a table, etc.

21. *Planetarium show*: A good activity if appropriate to the age level.

22. *Making ice cream.*

Arts and Crafts/Special Skills

Many books on children's crafts are available that give simple instructions for creative projects. Children enjoy crafts that they can complete and take home, or skills they can teach others.

1. *Feet-painting*: Have children paint the bottoms of their feet and walk on large sheets of paper—preferably on a basement floor.

2. *Woodship*: This makes a great father-son activity.

3. *Cornhusk dolls*: Older girls like this craft, but it needs ample time to complete. Younger girls enjoy dressing pre-made dolls with scraps of material, yarn, etc.

4. *Boats*: Small boats can be made of 2" x 4" blocks of wood, bike spokes, and paper sails. It's a great adventure to sail them on a stream or in a lake when completed.

5. *Candle-making.*

6. *Make animals* out of various kinds of nuts glued together.

7. *Make picture frames*: glue popsicle sticks together.

8. *Bookmarks*: Made on posterboard, decorated with magazine pictures, pressed flowers, colored paper, crayons, etc. These make great gifts. They can be preserved by covering with clear contact paper.

9. *Nature imprints.*

10. *Tissue-paper flowers.*

11. *Refrigerator magnets.*

12. *Rock-and-shell animals.*

13. *Flower baskets.*

14. *Finger-painting.*

15. *Decoupage flower pots.*

16. *Making puppets.*

17. *Making corsages.*

18. *Dried-flower arranging.*

19. *Making musical instruments.*

20. *Sponge-painting.*

21. *Making a banner.*

22. *"Rope day"*: Teach various skills and have activities using rope—knot-tying, lassoing, building a tire swing, tug-of-war, etc.

23. *Baking*: Girls especially love to bake and decorate a variety of delicacies. Baking works best if done in small groups, with enough utensils for everyone and chores for everyone to do. While food is baking, games can be played, songs sung, etc.

Special Events

Children love traditions. Annual events stir up excitement and anticipation, as well as instill continuity into any program. The following events can become traditional activities, or serve as fun one-time adventures.

1. *"Un-birthday" party*: This is a way to celebrate everyone's birthday at one time. It is a traditional birthday party, but with "un-birthday" games, cards, decorations, and food.

2. *Have older girls give a party for younger girls*: The older girls should plan it and conduct it, thus learning many skills and having fun at the same time.

3. *Big/little sister day or big/little brother day*: Teens or adults are paired one-to-one with younger children for a few hours of fun. Two or three pairs can do something together if desired. Some ideas: Go to a park, visit a zoo, play games, bake a cake, build a fort, etc.

4. *Sleepovers*: These are great fun for everyone, especially if the children themselves are involved in the planning.

5. *"School's Out" picnic*: At the end of the school year, have a picnic with all the families of children involved in the group. Center games and activities around the theme of summer approaching.

6. *Father-Son/Mother-Daughter sports events*: Basketball, volleyball, etc., can serve as an exciting way to have an event with the parents participating.

7. *Fund-raisers*: Bake sales, car washes, walkathons, etc., are all great fun for older children if they are involved in the planning and the work.

8. *Pizza party*: Either make your own or have the pizza delivered. In either case, it's sure to be a success!

9. *Mini-Olympics*: Children can rotate from one event to another, either keeping track of their own scores, or dividing into teams. Fifty-yard dash, broad jump, relays, obstacle courses, softball throw, and others can be used as events. This can be "jazzed up" as much as desired with homemade medals, cheers for each team, and even a facsimile of the Olympic torch. The more adults participating, the better. This takes planning, but will be a great event.

10. *Water festival*: Each child can bring a squirt gun, spray bottle, etc., and come dressed to get wet! All the games are centered around water (e.g., "squirt tag"). Even the refreshments should follow the theme (e.g., watermelon). Perfect for a hot summer day!

Alphabetical Index

Topical Index

DRAMATIC GAMES

ENCOURAGEMENT AND EDIFICATION GAMES

GETTING-TO-KNOW-EACH-OTHER GAMES

GUESSING GAMES

One Person Guesses

Word Guessing Games

HIDING GAMES

LARGE OPEN AREA GAMES

LAUGHTER GAMES

MEMORY GAMES

MUSICAL GAMES

TRADITIONAL SPORTS WITH A TWIST

Frisbee Games

TRIP GAMES

TRAVELING GAMES

TRUST GAMES

WATER AND "GETTING WET" GAMES

WORD GAMES